T0259688

SpringerBriefs in Computer Science

SpringerBriefs present concise summaries of cutting-edge research and practical applications across a wide spectrum of fields. Featuring compact volumes of 50 to 125 pages, the series covers a range of content from professional to academic. Typical topics might include:

- A timely report of state-of-the art analytical techniques
- A bridge between new research results, as published in journal articles, and a contextual literature review
- A snapshot of a hot or emerging topic
- An in-depth case study or clinical example
- A presentation of core concepts that students must understand in order to make independent contributions

Briefs allow authors to present their ideas and readers to absorb them with minimal time investment. Briefs will be published as part of Springer's eBook collection, with millions of users worldwide. In addition, Briefs will be available for individual print and electronic purchase. Briefs are characterized by fast, global electronic dissemination, standard publishing contracts, easy-to-use manuscript preparation and formatting guidelines, and expedited production schedules. We aim for publication 8–12 weeks after acceptance. Both solicited and unsolicited manuscripts are considered for publication in this series.

More information about this series at http://www.springer.com/series/10028

Ruipeng Gao · Fan Ye · Guojie Luo
Jason Cong

Smartphone-Based Indoor Map Construction

Principles and Applications

 Springer

Ruipeng Gao
Beijing Jiaotong University
Beijing
China

Fan Ye
Stony Brook University
Stony Brook, NY
USA

Guojie Luo
Peking University
Beijing
China

Jason Cong
UCLA
Los Angeles, CA
USA

ISSN 2191-5768   ISSN 2191-5776   (electronic)
SpringerBriefs in Computer Science
ISBN 978-981-10-8377-8   ISBN 978-981-10-8378-5   (eBook)
https://doi.org/10.1007/978-981-10-8378-5

Library of Congress Control Number: 2018934892

Printed on acid-free paper

This Springer imprint is published by the registered company Springer Nature Singapore Pte Ltd. part of Springer Nature
The registered company address is: 152 Beach Road, #21-01/04 Gateway East, Singapore 189721, Singapore

Preface

This book focuses on the ubiquitous indoor localization services by specifically addressing the issue of floor plans. It combines the computer vision algorithms and mobile techniques to reconstruct the complete and accurate floor plans, thus providing better location-based services for both humans and vehicles via commodity smartphones in indoor environments (e.g., a multilayer shopping mall with underground parking structures).

This book is based on Dr. Ruipeng Gao's PhD thesis co-supervised by Professors Jason Cong, Guojie Luo, and Fan Ye. The authors would like to thank the supports from NSFC 61702035 and PKU/UCLA Joint Research Institute of Science and Engineering.

Beijing, China   Ruipeng Gao
January 2018

Contents

1   **Introduction of Indoor Map Construction**   1
    1.1   Introduction   1
    Reference   2

2   **Indoor Map Construction via Mobile Crowdsensing**   3
    2.1   Introduction   3
    2.2   Design Overview   5
    2.3   Landmark Modeling   6
          2.3.1   The Landmark Model   6
          2.3.2   Coordinates of Geometric Vertices   8
          2.3.3   Connecting Points of Wall Segments   9
          2.3.4   Example   9
    2.4   Landmark Placement   10
          2.4.1   Notations   10
          2.4.2   Spatial Relation Acquisition   10
          2.4.3   Problem Formulation   12
          2.4.4   Optimization Algorithm   13
    2.5   Map Augmentation   14
          2.5.1   Wall Reconstruction   14
          2.5.2   Hallway Reconstruction   17
          2.5.3   Room Reconstruction   18
    2.6   Connection Area Detection   19
          2.6.1   Types of Connection Areas   19
          2.6.2   Features   21
          2.6.3   Unsupervised Classification   21
          2.6.4   Refinement and Placement   22
          2.6.5   Types of Connection Areas   22
    2.7   Performance   24

2.8   Discussion   26
2.9   Related Work   27
2.10   Conclusion   28
References   29

3   Incremental Indoor Map Construction with a Single User   31
3.1   Introduction   31
3.2   Overview   33
3.3   Localization via a Single Image...................   33
3.4   Trajectory Calibration and Cleaning...............   36
       3.4.1   Trajectory Calibration   37
       3.4.2   Trajectory Cleaning   38
3.5   Map Fusion Framework   39
       3.5.1   Dynamic Bayesian Network   39
       3.5.2   Particle Filter Algorithm..................   40
3.6   Landmark Recognition   42
3.7   Compartment Estimation.........................   43
3.8   Performance   45
3.9   Discussion   46
3.10   Related Work   47
3.11   Conclusion   48
References   48

4   Indoor Localization by Photo-Taking of the Environment   51
4.1   Introduction   51
4.2   Relative Position Measurement   54
4.3   Triangulation Method   57
       4.3.1   User Operations and Location Computation...........   57
       4.3.2   Criteria for Users to Choose Reference Objects   59
       4.3.3   Robustness of the Localization Primitive   60
4.4   Site Survey for Reference Objects Coordinates   63
       4.4.1   Location Estimation in Unmapped Environments   64
       4.4.2   Experiments on Site Survey   65
4.5   Identifying Chosen Reference Objects   66
       4.5.1   System Architecture and Workflow................   67
4.6   Benchmark Selection of Reference Objects   69
       4.6.1   Benchmark Selection Problem   69
       4.6.2   NP-Completeness Proof   70
       4.6.3   A Heuristic Algorithm   71
4.7   Improve Localization with Geographical Constraints..........   72
       4.7.1   Experiment Results and Problems in Early Prototype   73
       4.7.2   Geographical Constraints   74
       4.7.3   System Localization Performance   75
4.8   Discussion   76

4.9	Related Work	77
4.10	Conclusion	78
References		79

5 Smartphone-Based Real-Time Vehicle Tracking in Indoor Parking Structures 81
5.1	Introduction	81
5.2	Design Overview	84
5.3	Trajectory Tracing	85
	5.3.1 Conventional Approaches	85
	5.3.2 Shadow Trajectory Tracing	86
	5.3.3 Equivalence Proof	88
5.4	Real-Time Tracking	92
	5.4.1 Intuition	92
	5.4.2 Road Skeleton Model	93
	5.4.3 Probabilistic Tracking Framework	94
	5.4.4 Tracking Algorithms	95
5.5	Landmark Detection	98
	5.5.1 Types of Landmarks	98
	5.5.2 Feature and Classification Algorithm	100
	5.5.3 Prediction and Rollback	101
5.6	Performance	101
5.7	Discussion	104
5.8	Related Work	105
5.9	Conclusions	107
References		107

Chapter 1
Introduction of Indoor Map Construction

Abstract We describe the motivation and background of map construction for ubiquitous indoor location-based services, and then give an overview of this book and present how it is organized in the following chapters.

1.1 Introduction

In contrast to the almost ubiquitous coverage outdoors, localization service is at best sporadic indoors. The industry state-of-the-art Google Indoor Maps [1] as of 2017, covers 10,000 locations worldwide, which is only a small fraction of millions of indoor environments (e.g., airports, train stations, shopping malls, museums, and hospitals) on the Earth. The lack of indoor maps is a fundamental obstacle to ubiquitous indoor location-based services. Service providers have to conduct effort-intensive and time-consuming business negotiations with building owners or operators to collect the floor plans, or wait for them to voluntarily upload such data. Neither is conducive to large-scale coverage in short time.

Recently, some academic work has made admirable progress to automatic indoor map construction. They require only commodity mobile devices (e.g., smartphones); thus, can achieve scalable construction by crowdsensing data from many users. Despite such progress, they usually require inertial and WiFi data, which are inherently noisy thus difficult to produce precise and detailed maps.

In this book, we leverage both mobile and vision data via commodity smartphones to construct the floor plans of complex indoor environments. It avoids the intensive efforts and time overhead in the business negotiation process for service providers. They do not need to talk to building owners/operators one by one, or hire dedicated personnel to measure indoor environments inch by inch. It opens up the possibility of fast and scalable floor plan reconstruction.

After a comprehensive review of scene reconstruction methods, this book produces accurate geometric information of each landmark from images and derives landmarks spatial relationship and the rough sketches of accessible areas with inertial and WiFi data for less computing overhead. Then, recent novel findings from the authors are presented in detail, including the optimization and probabilistic formulations for more solid foundations and better robustness to combat errors, sev-

© The Author(s) 2018
R. Gao et al., *Smartphone-Based Indoor Map Construction*,
SpringerBriefs in Computer Science, https://doi.org/10.1007/978-981-10-8378-5_1

eral new approaches to promote the current sporadic availability of indoor location-based services, and a holistic solution from floor plan reconstruction to indoor localization, tracking, and navigation. Our new approaches are designed for different types of indoor environments (e.g., shopping malls, office buildings and labs) and different users.

Our design is based on the realization that computer vision and mobile techniques have complementary strengths. The vision techniques can produce accurate geometric information when the area has stable and distinct visual features. They are suitable for landmarks where logos, decorations constitute rich features, and detailed information about their positions/orientations are desired. The mobile techniques give only rough sketches of accessible areas with much lower computing overhead, which are suitable for in-between sections such as textureless or glass walls where much fewer stable features exist, while less detailed information is required. Therefore, we leverage "expensive" vision techniques to obtain more accurate and detailed information about individual landmarks, and use "cheap" inertial data to obtain the placement of landmarks on a large, common floor plane, and derive the less critical hallway and room information at lower fidelity. The optimization and probabilistic formulations give us more solid foundations and better robustness to combat errors from data.

The reconstructed indoor maps can significantly improve the indoor location-based services, both for pedestrians and drivers in indoor environments. With the reconstructed maps, we explore alternative indoor localization approaches which have comparable performance but without relying on the RF signature. Specifically, we leverage environmental *landmarks* (indoor places of interests, such as logos of stores, paintings on the walls, or bumps in the parking structure), and users use the smartphone to measure their relative positions to those landmarks, and the coordinates of the reference landmarks are used to compute user locations. This has a few advantages: (1) Landmarks are part of the environment and abundant; they do not require dedicated deployment and maintenance efforts like IT infrastructure; (2) they seldom move and usually remain static over long periods of time. They are not affected by and thus impervious to electromagnetic disturbances from microwaves, cordless phones, or wireless cameras. Once measured, their coordinates usually do not change, thus eliminating the need for periodic recalibration.

The rest of this book is organized as follows: First, we present two methods to construct complete indoor floor plans automatically, and then give two examples on how the produced maps improve indoor location-based services. Specifically, Chap. 2 leverages the crowdsensed data from mobile users and constructs the floor plan as a batch processing system, and Chap. 3 generates it incrementally from a single user. With the reconstructed maps, Chap. 4 localizes pedestrians in the building without RF signals, and Chap. 5 tracks vehicles in real time in parking structures.

Reference

1. Google Indoor Maps Availability, http://support.google.com/gmm/bin/answer.py?hl=en&answer=1685827

Chapter 2
Indoor Map Construction via Mobile Crowdsensing

Abstract The lack of indoor maps is a critical reason behind the current sporadic availability of indoor localization service. Service providers have to go through effort-intensive and time-consuming business negotiations with building operators, or hire dedicated personnel to gather such data. In this chapter, we propose Jigsaw, a floor plan reconstruction system that leverages crowdsensed data from mobile users. It extracts the position, size, and orientation information of individual landmark objects from images taken by users. It also obtains the spatial relation between adjacent landmark objects from inertial sensor data, and then computes the coordinates and orientations of these objects on an initial floor plan. By combining user mobility traces and locations where images are taken, it produces complete floor plans with hallway connectivity, room sizes, and shapes. It also identifies different types of connection areas (e.g., escalators, stairs) between stories, and employs a refinement algorithm to correct detection errors. Our experiments on three stories of two large shopping malls show that the 90-percentile errors of positions and orientations of landmark objects are about $1 \sim 2$ m and $5 \sim 9°$, while the hallway connectivity and connection areas between stories are 100% correct.

2.1 Introduction

Online digital maps (e.g., Google Maps) have provided great convenience for location-based services (LBS) outdoors such as finding nearby point-of-interests (POIs) and navigation. However, for indoor environments where people spend over 80% of the time [1], such maps are extremely scarce and unavailable in most buildings. This has become a huge obstacle to pervasive indoor LBS.

Accurate indoor floor plan construction at low costs is urgently needed. Autonomous robots equipped with high-precision special sensors (e.g., laser rangers [2], depth cameras [3], sonars [4]) can produce high-quality maps. However, the high manufacturing costs, operational, and logistic obstacles make it difficult to deploy robots in large quantities.

In this chapter, we propose *Jigsaw* [5], which leverages crowdsensed data from mobile users to construct the floor plans of complex indoor environments. It avoids

R. Gao et al., *Smartphone-Based Indoor Map Construction*,
SpringerBriefs in Computer Science, https://doi.org/10.1007/978-981-10-8378-5_2

the intensive effort and time overhead in the business negotiation process for service providers. They do not need to talk to building owners/operators one by one, or hire dedicated personnel to measure indoor environments inch by inch. Jigsaw opens up the possibility of fast and scalable floor plan reconstruction.

The concept of mobile crowdsensing [6] has become increasingly popular. Recent work has used crowdsensed data to localize users [7] and reduce the calibration efforts of WiFi signatures [8, 9]. Among others [10–13], CrowdInside [14] pioneers the efforts of constructing hallway/room shape and connectivity of floor plans. It uses inertial data to build and combine user mobility traces to derive the approximate shape of accessible areas of floor plans.

Nevertheless, there exists much space for improvements. Inertial data do not give the accurate coordinates and orientations of indoor places of interests (POIs, such as store entrances in shopping malls, henceforth called *landmarks*), which are critical to guide users. Due to error accumulation in dead reckoning, "anchor points" (e.g., entrances/exits of elevators/escalators/ stairs and locations with GPS reception) with unique sensing data signatures are needed to correct the drift in mobile traces. But in many large indoor environments, such anchor points can be too sparse to provide sufficient correction. Therefore, both over- and underestimation of accessible areas can easily happen, e.g., when a trace drifts into walls, or there exist corners users seldom walk into.

Jigsaw combines computer vision and mobile techniques, and uses optimization and probabilistic formulations to build relatively complete and accurate floor plans. We use computer vision techniques to extract geometric features (e.g., widths of store entrances, lengths, and orientations of adjoining walls) of individual landmarks from images. We then design several types of data-gathering *micro-tasks*, each a series of actions that users can take to collect data specifically useful for building floor plans. We derive the relative spatial relationship between adjacent landmarks from inertial data of some types of micro-tasks, and compute the optimal coordinates and orientations of landmarks on a common floor plane. Then, user mobility traces from another type of micro-task are used to obtain the hallway connectivity, orientation, and room shapes/sizes, using combinatorial optimization and probabilistic occupancy techniques. After reconstruction of each single-story floor plan, inertial data and WiFi/cellular signatures and images are also used to detect different types of connection areas between stories (e.g., stairs, escalators, and elevators) to finally produce a multistory floor plan.

We make the following contributions in this work:

- We identify suitable computer vision techniques and design a *landmark modeling* algorithm that takes their output from landmark images to derive the coordinates of major geometry features (e.g., store entrances and adjoining wall segments) and camera poses in their local coordinate systems.
- We design micro-tasks to measure the spatial relationship between landmarks, and devise a *landmark placement* algorithm that uses a maximum likelihood estimation (MLE) formulation to compute the optimal coordinates, orientations of landmarks on a common floor plane.

- We devise several *augmentation algorithms* that reconstruct wall boundaries using a combinatorial optimization formulation, and obtain hallway connectivity and orientation, room size/shape using probabilistic occupancy maps that are robust to noises in mobile user traces. We also reconstruct three types of connection areas between different floors and general multistory floor plans.
- We develop a prototype and conduct extensive experiments in three stories of two large complex indoor environments. The results show that the position and orientation errors of landmarks are about $1 \sim 2$ m and $5° \sim 9°$ at 90-percentile, with 100% correct isle topology connectivity and connection areas between stories, which demonstrate the effectiveness of our design.

Note that we do not claim novelty in developing new computer vision techniques. Our main contribution is the identification and combination of appropriate vision and mobile techniques in new ways suitable for floor plan construction, and accompanying mathematical formulations and solutions that yield much improved accuracy despite errors and noises from image and inertial data sources.

The rest of this chapter is organized as follows: We give an overview (Sect. 2.2), and then present the design of the landmark modeling, placement, and augmentation algorithms (Sects. 2.3, 2.4, 2.5 and 2.6). We also conduct an experimental evaluation of our design and demonstrate its effectiveness in Sect. 5.6. After a discussion (Sect. 2.8) of limitations, comparison to related work (Sect. 2.9), we conclude the chapter (Sect. 2.10).

2.2 Design Overview

Similar to existing work [10–14], Jigsaw requires data collected using commodity smartphones from users. We assume that upon proper incentives (e.g., cash rewards [15, 16]), users willing to conduct simple *micro-tasks* can be recruited. They will follow guidelines and gather data in required form and manner: e.g., taking a single photo of a store entrance; taking a photo of one store and then spinning the body to take a photo of another store; walking a certain trajectory on the floor or across stories while taking a photo immediately before/after the walk. Such micro-tasks allow us to gather data for specific elements in floor maps. Given successful industrial precedences [15, 16] where users accomplish tasks in exchange for rewards, and plenty of research [17] on how incentives influence user behavior, we argue such a paradigm is feasible and practical. We leave the exact design of incentive form as future work.

Jigsaw utilizes images, acceleration, and gyroscope data. The reconstruction consists of three stages: landmark modeling, placement, and augmentation (Fig. 2.1). First, two computer vision techniques, structure from motion (SfM) [18] and vanishing line detection [19], are used to obtain the sizes and coordinates of major geometry measurements of each landmark in its local coordinate system (Sect. 2.3). SfM also produces the location and orientation of the camera for each image, effectively local-

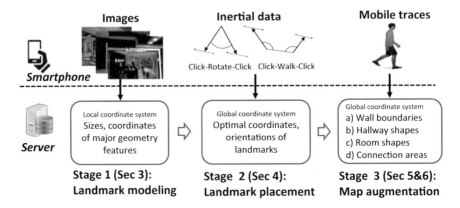

Fig. 2.1 Jigsaw contains three stages: landmark modeling, landmark placement, and map augmentation. Each stage uses image or inertial data and output from the previous stage

izing the user who took the picture. Next, two types of micro-tasks, Click-Rotate-Click (CRC) and Click-Walk-Click (CWC), are used to gather gyroscope and acceleration data to measure the distances and orientation differences between landmarks. The measurements are used as constraints in an MLE formulation to compute the most likely coordinates and orientations of landmarks in a global coordinate system (Sect. 2.4). Then, a combinatorial optimization is used to connect landmarks' adjoining wall segments into continuous boundaries, and probabilistic occupancy maps are used to obtain hallway connectivity, orientation, and room sizes/shapes from inertial user traces (Sect. 2.5). Finally, inertial data with images and WiFi/cellular signatures are used to identify connection areas between stories, and a refinement algorithm is employed to correct detection errors; thus, we generate the multistory floor plan (Sect. 2.6).

2.3   Landmark Modeling

In this section, we describe how we extract sizes and coordinates of major geometry features (e.g., widths of store entrances, lengths/orientations of adjoining walls) of landmarks from their images.

2.3.1   The Landmark Model

We use a very simple model to describe the major geometry features of a landmark. As illustrated in Fig. 2.2, a landmark is denoted by $L = (P, Q)$, where P are the main geometric vertices of the landmark (e.g., the four corners $P_1 \sim P_4$ of a store

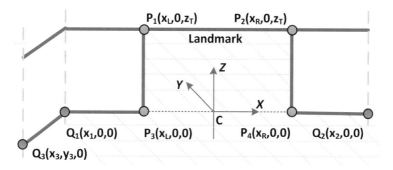

Fig. 2.2 The model of this exemplary store entrance has four geometric vertices $P_1 \sim P_4$ and three connecting points of wall segments $Q_1 \sim Q_3$ in its local coordinate system

entrance), and Q are connecting points of adjoining wall segments on the floor (e.g., $Q_1 \sim Q_3$ for two wall segments). Each landmark has a local coordinate system, and we place its origin C at the center of the store's entrance line $\overline{P_3 P_4}$. The X-axis is colinear with $\overrightarrow{C P_4}$, the X-Y plane is the ground floor, and the three axes follow the right-hand rule.

We leverage the output of two computer vision techniques, Structure from Motion (SfM) [18] and vanishing line detection [19], to obtain the coordinates of P, Q from landmark images.

Structure from motion is a mature computer vision technique commonly used to construct the 3D models of an object. Given a set of images of the same object (e.g., a building) from different viewpoints, it produces: (1) a "point cloud" consisting of many points in a local 3D coordinate system. Each point represents a physical point on the object,[1] and (2) the pose (i.e., 3D coordinates and orientations) of the camera for each image, which effectively localizes the camera/user taking that image.

Using SfM only and as-is, however, may not be the best match for indoor floor plan reconstruction. First, SfM relies on large numbers of evenly distributed stable and distinctive image features for detailed and accurate 3D model reconstruction. Although landmarks themselves usually enjoy rich features due to logos, decorations, many in-between sections have too few (e.g., textureless walls), interior (e.g., transparent glass walls) or dynamic (e.g., moving customers) features, which SfM may not handle well. Second, the "point cloud" produced by SfM is not what we need for constructing floor maps. We still have to derive the coordinates of those geometric features in our model, e.g., the corners of an entrance.

---

[1]To be more exact, each point represents a "feature point" as detected by certain feature extractor algorithms (e.g., SIFT [20]).

2.3.2 Coordinates of Geometric Vertices

To obtain the coordinates of major geometry vertices needed in the model, we explore a two-phase algorithm. First, we use an existing vanishing line detection algorithm [19] to produce line segments for each image of the same landmark (Fig. 2.3b). We merge colinear and parallel segments close to each other into long line segments (Fig. 2.3b). This method is done using an intersection angle threshold and a distance threshold between two line segments, and both thresholds are set empirically. The merging is repeated for all line segment pairs until no further merging is possible. We filter out the remaining short segments and leave only the long ones.

Next, we project merged 2D long lines from each image back into the 3D coordinate system using transformation matrices produced by SfM [18]. We then use an adapted k-means algorithm to cluster the projected 3D lines into groups according to their distance in 3D and merge each cluster into a 3D line segment. This gives the likely 3D contour lines of the landmark. The intersection points of them are computed for major geometry vertices.

One practical issue that the above algorithm addresses is images taken from relatively extreme angles. Long contour lines (e.g., $\overline{P_1 P_2}$ in Fig. 2.2) may become a short segment on such pictures. Because the majority of images are taken more or less front and center, real contour lines will have sufficient numbers of long line segments after the merging and projection. Thus, the second phase clustering can identify them while removing "noises" from images of extreme angles.

Due to the same reason, we find that the coordinates of wall segment connecting points farther from the center are not as accurate. This is simply because most images would cover the center of the landmark (e.g., store entrance) but may miss some peripheral areas farther away. Next, we use a more reliable method to derive coordinates of wall connecting points.

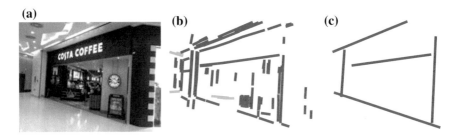

Fig. 2.3 Geometric vertices detection workflow: **a** original image, **b** detect line segments parallel to the three orthogonal axes, and **c** merged long line segments corresponding to the landmark's major contour lines. Different colors represent different dimensions

2.3.3 Connecting Points of Wall Segments

We project the 3D point cloud of the landmark onto the floor plane and search for densely distributed points in a line shape to find wall segments and their connecting points. This is because the projection of feature points on the same vertical plane/wall would fall onto the joining line to the floor (e.g., $\overline{P_3 Q_1}$ of the wall segment adjoining the entrance on left).

We start from some geometry vertices computed previously (e.g., $\overline{P_3 P_4}$ gives the projected line of the entrance wall in Fig. 2.2, marked as two diamonds in Fig. 2.4), and then find the two ends (e.g., marked as two crosses in Fig. 2.4) of this wall. From each end, the search for the next connecting point continues, until no lines consisting of densely distributed points can be found. Figure 2.4 shows three wall connecting points discovered.

2.3.4 Example

Figure 2.4 shows the point cloud of one store entrance projected onto the floor plane and SfM produced camera locations. We mark the geometry vertices (diamonds) and the wall connecting points (crosses). In this example, the width of the entrance has an error of 0.086 m (4.78% of the actual width 1.8 m). We also detect two external wall segments along the hallway, and their intersection angle error is 0.08° out of 90° (0.09%). We find that the 176 camera locations produced by SfM (only some of them are shown) are quite accurate. The localization error is within 1.2 m at 90% percentile, and maximum error is 1.5 m. We also test how the number of images

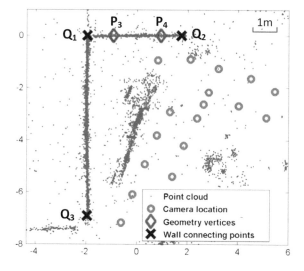

Fig. 2.4 A landmark's point cloud projected to the floor plan, with camera locations, critical contour line (P_3 and P_4), and connecting points of wall segments (Q_1, Q_2, and Q_3)

impacts SfM's localization performance. As we vary the number of photos from 20 to 160, we find that about 80 images are sufficient for camera localization: 75 (94%) images are localized, with 90% error of 1.8 m and maximum error of 5.2 m. We will present more systematic evaluation results in Sect. 2.7.

2.4 Landmark Placement

In this section, we estimate the *configuration* of landmarks, which is defined as the coordinates and orientations of landmarks in the global 2D coordinate system. We also derive the global coordinates of locations where photos are taken. To this end, we first obtain the spatial relationship between adjacent landmarks from inertial and image data. The determination of the configuration is formulated as an optimization problem that finds the most likely coordinates and orientations of landmarks that achieve the maximal consistency with those pairwise relationship observations.

Once the landmarks' global coordinates are known, the global positions where photos are taken is a simple coordination transformation of the camera location in each landmark's local coordinate system (described in Sect. 2.3) to the global one. Such camera positions play an important role in the *augmentation algorithm* for the occupancy map in Sect. 2.5.

2.4.1 Notations

Suppose there are n local coordinate systems corresponding to n landmarks l_1, $l_2, ..., l_n$. $X_i = (x_i, y_i) \in \mathbb{R}^2$ and $\phi_i \in [-\pi, \pi)$ are the x-y coordinates and orientation of landmark l_i in the global coordinate system, respectively. $\theta = (X, \phi)$ is the configuration of landmarks to be determined, where $X = (X_1, ..., X_n)$, $\phi = (\phi_1, ..., \phi_n)$.

$R_i = R(\phi_i) = \begin{bmatrix} cos\phi_i & -sin\phi_i \\ sin\phi_i & cos\phi_i \end{bmatrix}$ is the rotation matrix used in coordinate transformation between the global and local coordinate systems of landmark l_i. $X_j^i = (x_j^i, y_j^i) = R(\phi_i)^T (X_j - X_i)$ and $\phi_j^i = \phi_j - \phi_i$ are the x-y coordinates and orientation of landmark l_j in the local coordinate system of landmark l_i, respectively.

2.4.2 Spatial Relation Acquisition

The spatial relationship between two adjacent landmarks l_i, l_j are X_j^i and ϕ_j^i, the coordinates and orientation of landmark l_j in the local coordinate system of landmark l_i (or vice versa, illustrated in Fig. 2.5). It is difficult to obtain such measurements

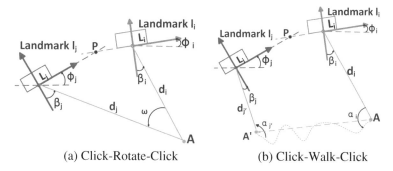

(a) Click-Rotate-Click   (b) Click-Walk-Click

Fig. 2.5 Micro-tasks: A is where two photos of landmark l_i and l_j are taken in CRC. (d_i, β_i) are the length of AL_i, and the angle formed by line AL_i and normal direction of L_i, respectively. P is the intersection point of the two x-axes of the two local coordinate systems. A' is where the walk ends in CWC

directly from users because they do not carry tools such as tapes. We design two data-gathering micro-tasks where the user takes a few actions to gather inertial and image data, from which we compute the pairwise relationship observations.

Click-Rotate-Click (CRC): In this micro-task, a user clicks to take a photo of a landmark l_i from position A (shown in Fig. 2.5a), and then spins the body and camera for a particular angle (e.g., ω degrees) to take another photo of a second landmark l_j. The angle ω can be obtained quite accurately from the gyroscope [7, 8].

(d_i, β_i) represents the distance between camera A and landmark l_i, and the angle formed by line $L_i A$ and the normal line of landmark l_i, respectively. They can be derived from the camera pose (i.e., coordinates and orientation in $l_i's$ location coordinate system) as produced by SfM (Sect. 2.3). Similar is (d_j, β_j). P represents the intersection point of the two x-axes in the two landmarks' local coordinate systems.

From plane geometry, quadrangle $AL_i PL_j$ is uniquely determined given (d_i, β_i), (d_j, β_j) and ω. Thus, we can calculate an observation of one landmark's coordinates and orientation in the other's local coordinate system (and vice versa), namely, observations of (ϕ_j^i, X_j^i), (ϕ_i^j, X_i^j) denoted as (O_j^i, Z_j^i) and (O_i^j, Z_i^j).

Click-Walk-Click (CWC): In this micro-task, a user clicks to take a photo of landmark l_i, and then walks to another location A' to take another photo of a second landmark l_j (shown in Fig. 2.5b). It is useful when two landmarks are farther away and finding one location to take proper photos for both is difficult. The distance $|AA'|$ could be calculated from step counting method [8], and the angle between the direction when user takes a photo and his/her walking direction, i.e., (α_i, α_j') at two locations A and A', could be obtained from placement offset estimation method [21] and gyroscope readings. Measurements calculation here is similar to that of Click-Rotate-Click except that the quadrangle is replaced by a pentagon as illustrated in Fig. 2.5a.

The two camera locations in CWC can be used as "anchor points" to calibrate the trace. Due to well-known error accumulation [14] in inertial tracking, many methods

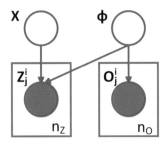

Fig. 2.6 Bayesian belief network representation of our problem. X is the coordinates while ϕ is the orientations of all the landmarks. $\theta = (X, \phi)$ is the hidden variable we need to estimate based on measurements. Z_j^i, O_j^i measures the coordinates and orientation of landmark j in the coordinates system of landmark i. Measurements of each kind are aggregated together with the total number of that kind denoted by n_Z, n_O

use anchor points (places of known locations such as entrances/exits of escalators, elevators, stairs) to pinpoint the trace on the floor. In environments with large open space, such anchor points may be sparse. CWC addresses the sparsity issue because users can take photos almost anywhere.

Nevertheless, we use CWC between two landmarks only when CRC is difficult to conduct, because the accuracy of step counting-based inertial tracking is limited compared to that of the gyroscope in CRC. Jigsaw utilizes both types of measurements while considering their varying qualities, by assigning different confidences to each type in a common optimization problem (described next in Sect. 2.4.3).

2.4.3 Problem Formulation

We use maximum likelihood estimation (MLE) to formulate the optimal configuration problem. Our problem is represented as a Bayesian belief network (Fig. 2.6) describing the conditional dependence structure among variables (denoted as nodes), where each variable only directly depends on its predecessors.

We denote the maximum likelihood estimation of θ as θ^*. The intuition for maximizing $P(Z, O|X, \phi)$ is that we try to find a configuration of landmarks $\theta^* = (X^*, \phi^*)$ under which those measurements Z, O (i.e., observations of X, ϕ) are most likely to be observed.

We have the following equations based on the conditional dependence in the graphical model:

$$\theta^* = \arg\max_{\theta} P(Z, O|X, \phi) = \arg\max_{\theta} P(O|\phi)P(Z|\phi, X)$$

$$= \arg\min_{\theta} -\sum_{O_j^i} \log P(O_j^i|\phi) - \sum_{Z_j^i} \log P(Z_j^i|\phi, X).$$

As is standard in probabilistic mapping literature [22], we assume Gaussian measurement models that give further transformation into

$$\theta^* = \arg\min_{\theta} \sum_{O_j^i} \frac{\|\phi_j^i - O_j^i\|^2}{\sigma_O^2} + \sum_{Z_j^i} \frac{\|X_j^i - Z_j^i\|^2}{\lambda_Z^2}, \qquad (2.1)$$

where σ_O, λ_Z are covariances of normally distributed zero-mean measurement noises for different kinds of measurements. As noted in Sect. 2.4.2, we assign small σ_O, λ_Z for CRC measurements to give them predominance over those of CWC.

Without losing generality, we can simply use variable substitution to yield an equivalent nonlinear least squares formulation:

$$\underset{\phi, X}{\text{minimize}} \quad \sum_{O_j^i} \|\phi_j^i - O_j^i\|^2 + \sum_{Z_j^i} \|X_j^i - Z_j^i\|^2. \qquad (2.2)$$

The intuition is that we try to find a configuration of landmarks $\theta^* = (X^*, \phi^*)$ such that the aggregate difference between ϕ_j^i, X_j^i derived from (X^*, ϕ^*) and their measurements O_j^i, Z_j^i is minimized.

2.4.4 Optimization Algorithm

Let's denote problem (2.2) as

$$\underset{\phi, X}{\text{minimize}} \quad f(\phi) + g(\phi, X) \qquad (2.3)$$

since the two terms in (2.2) are functions of ϕ and (ϕ, X).

Careful examination [23] shows that each term in $g(\phi, X)$ is linear square of X; thus, $g(\phi, X)$ is a typical linear least squares of X with a closed-form solution. We denote the minimum as $h(\phi)$. Thus, problem (2.3) is equivalent to

$$\underset{\phi}{\text{minimize}} \quad f(\phi) + h(\phi). \qquad (2.4)$$

We solve this problem based on an observation: minimizing $f(\phi)$ gives the most likely orientation ϕ' of landmarks with orientation relationship observations only. Due to relatively accurate gyroscope data, ϕ' would be very close to the global optimal ϕ^* that minimizes $f(\phi) + h(\phi)$. Thus, we find the optimum of $f(\phi)$ as the initial value, and then use stochastic gradient descent (SGD) to find the global minimum ϕ^*.

STEP 1: Find ϕ' given measurements O.

$$\underset{\phi}{\text{minimize}} \quad f(\boldsymbol{\phi}) = \sum_{O_j^i} \|\phi_j^i - O_j^i\|^2 \tag{2.5}$$

Note that this is not a linear least squares problem since the result of the subtraction on angles is periodic with a period of 2π. What adds to the difficulty is the loop dependence of the orientations of different landmarks. The effect of adjusting the orientation of one landmark would propagate along pairwise relationship observations, eventually back to itself.

We solve this problem as follows: First, we find the maximum spanning tree of the orientation dependence graph where edges are relationship observations between landmarks. This problem $f_{MST}(\boldsymbol{\phi})$ can be easily solved because adjusting the orientation of one landmark has a one-way effect on its decedents only. Again, due to the accuracy of gyroscope and relatively small number of removed edges (i.e., relationship observations), the resulting ϕ'_{MST} would be in near neighborhood of the true optimum ϕ'. Then we perform gradient descent from ϕ'_{MST} find a minimum likely to be ϕ'. In reality, we do find them are usually in the close neighborhood.

STEP 2: Perform stochastic gradient descent (SGD) from ϕ' to find ϕ^*. Based on the intuition explained earlier that ϕ' is close to ϕ^*, we perform SGD which is known to be able to climb out of "local minima" to find the global minimum with higher probability.

2.5 Map Augmentation

After obtaining the optimal coordinates and orientations of the landmarks, we need more details for a relatively complete floor plan: (1) wall reconstruction for external boundaries of the hallway, (2) hallway structure, and (3) rough shapes of rooms. Next, we describe how to construct such details.

2.5.1 Wall Reconstruction

Connecting wall segments between adjacent landmarks in manners "most consistent" with the likely architectural structure of buildings is not trivial. Naive methods such as using a convex hull to cover all segments produce an external boundary but may not connect those segments "inside" the hull (Fig. 2.7b).

To formally define the problem, we represent a wall segment as a line segment with its normal direction pointing to the hallway and denote the endpoints on its left/right side as L and R (shown in Fig. 2.8). Therefore, k wall segments have two

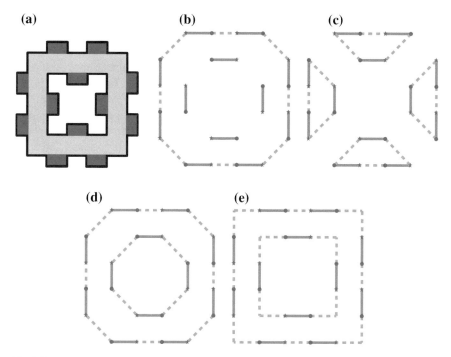

Fig. 2.7 Comparison between different algorithms: **a** example scenario, **b** convex hull of all wall segments, **c** one possible output of the greedy method, **d** minimal weight matching using distance as weight, and **e** our minimal weight matching method

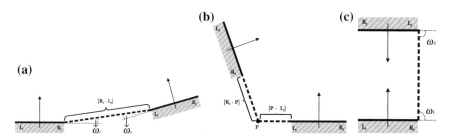

Fig. 2.8 Given the normal direction pointing to the hallway, two endpoints of a wall segment are labeled L and R. New wall segments must link endpoints with different labels. Three cases of connection are shown: **a** two nearly collinear segments, **b** two nearly perpendicular segments, and **c** two nearly opposite segments

sets of endpoints $L = \{L_1, L_2, ..., L_k\}$ and $R = \{R_1, R_2, ..., R_k\}$. We need to add new wall segments connecting each endpoint in L to one in R.

Every possible solution corresponds to a perfect matching π, where π is a permutation of $(1, 2, ..., k)$, indicating $L(i)$ and $R(\pi(i))$ are linked for $i = 1, 2, ..., k$.

Thus, the problem becomes a combinatorial optimization problem that finds the perfect matching with the minimal weight (i.e., most likely connection manner) in a bipartite graph.

A simple greedy algorithm uses distance as weight and connects every endpoint in set L to the closest (i.e., least distance) one in set R directly. The drawback is that the result depends on the order of connecting endpoints, and 90° corners commonly seen in buildings may be missing. For example, Fig. 2.7c and d shows two possible results, where one is incorrect while the other does not have 90° corners.

To address the above issues, we consider the two following options for linking two adjacent wall segments. Each option carries a weight, which can be computed given two endpoints in L and R. The weight represents the likelihood of the option: a smaller one indicates a more likely linking manner.

Linking with another segment directly. Two segments (L_i, R_i) and (L_j, R_j) are linked by another segment between L_i and R_j directly. The weight is defined as

$$w_{ij}^{(1)} = |R_i - L_j|(\omega_1 + \omega_2), \tag{2.6}$$

where $|R_i - L_j|$ is the distance between two endpoints R_i and L_j and ω_1, ω_2 are the turning angles from segments (L_i, R_i), (L_j, R_j) to the newly added segment (illustrated in Fig. 2.8a and c). Such direct linking is more likely when two adjacent segments are collinear or facing each other.

Extending to an intersection. If the two segments are not parallel, extending them from endpoints R_i and L_j reaches a point of intersection. This is another possibility and its weight is defined as

$$w_{ij}^{(2)} = \frac{|R_i - P| + |P - L_j|}{2}, \tag{2.7}$$

where P is the point of intersection and $|R_i - P|$ and $|P - L_j|$ are the distances among them (illustrated in Fig. 2.8b). For two (close to) perpendicular segments, the above equation produces a smaller weight, ensuring proper connection for 90° corners.

Given the configuration of landmarks estimated in Sect. 2.4, we calculate $w_{ij}^{(1)}$ and $w_{ij}^{(2)}$ for each pair of wall segments based on (2.6) and (2.7). We define the weight w_{ij} of linking L_i and R_j as the smaller of the two:

$$w_{ij} = \begin{cases} \min{(w_{ij}^{(1)}, w_{ij}^{(2)})}, & i \neq j; \\ \infty, & i = j. \end{cases} \tag{2.8}$$

the weight is ∞ if $i = j$ since the two endpoints of the same segment is already connected.

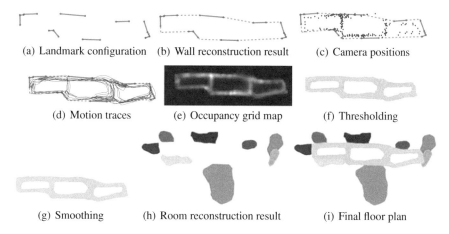

(a) Landmark configuration   (b) Wall reconstruction result   (c) Camera positions

(d) Motion traces   (e) Occupancy grid map   (f) Thresholding

(g) Smoothing   (h) Room reconstruction result   (i) Final floor plan

Fig. 2.9 Augmentation process: **a** shows landmark configuration results. **b** Depicts hallway external boundary after wall reconstruction. **c** and **d** Show camera positions and motion traces. Combining the above, occupancy grid map is shown in **e**, followed by thresholding (**f**) and smoothing (**g**). **h** Depicts room reconstruction results, and the final floor plan is shown in **i**

Given all the weights, we can find the perfect matching π^* to minimize the total weight as follows:

$$\underset{\pi}{\text{minimize}} \quad \sum_{i=1}^{k} w_{i\pi(i)}. \tag{2.9}$$

While a naive exhaustive search needs factorial time, we recognize that finding the perfect matching with minimal weight in a bipartite graph can be solved efficiently by Kuhn–Munkres algorithm [24] in polynomial time ($O(n^3)$) where n is the number of landmarks, which is usually a small number (e.g., tens of stores for one floor of a mall). Figure 2.7e shows the correct result produced by our algorithm, and Fig. 2.9b illustrates the outcome in a real environment.

2.5.2 Hallway Reconstruction

To reconstruct the structure of the whole hallway, we first build the occupancy grid map [25], which is a dominant paradigm for environment modeling in mobile robotics. Occupancy grid map represents environments by fine-grained grid cells each with a variable representing the probability that the cell is accessible.

In Jigsaw, it can be regarded as a confidence map that reflects the positions accessible to people. This confidence map is initialized as a matrix full of zeros. We add confidence to a cell if there is evidence that it is accessible, and the scale of the confidence we add depends on how much we trust the evidence. We fuse three kinds of cues to reconstruct the occupancy grid map.

External boundary of the hallway: This is reconstructed in Sect. 2.5.1. Due to obstacles (e.g., indoor plants placed next to the wall), the accessible positions are not equivalent to the region bounded by the external boundary. Since the area in front of landmarks is often the entrance, it is always accessible and we assign higher confidence. Places in front of a newly added wall are usually accessible but obstacles may exist. Thus, we assign less confidence to such places.

Positions of cameras: Positions of cameras can be computed given the configuration of landmarks and the relative position between cameras and landmarks. Such positions are obviously accessible. So we add confidence to places around every camera's position. Figure 2.9c depicts positions of cameras with the result of wall reconstruction.

Motion traces in the hallway: The shape of motion traces can be computed using methods such as [8, 21]. The traces can be calibrated by taking photos and using their locations as anchor points. Given such information, we can correct the step length, which is one primary source of error in step counting-based tracking. Such traces in the hallway add confidence to positions along them. Because motion traces usually carry higher errors, we assign less confidence along motion traces comparing to positions of cameras. Figure 2.9d depicts motion traces in the hallway with the result of wall reconstruction.

The final occupancy grid map is shown in Fig. 2.9e. We use an automatic threshold-based binarization technique [26] to determine whether each cell is accessible, thus creating a binary map indicating which cells are accessible. The accumulation of evidences makes our method robust to noises and outliers in crowdsensed input: a cell is considered accessible only when there is enough evidence. The result of thresholding is depicted in Fig. 2.9f. To further improve the result, we implement a smoothing algorithm based on *alpha-shape* [14], which is a generalization of the concept of convex hull. Figure 2.9g shows the final result of hallway reconstruction after smoothing.

2.5.3 Room Reconstruction

We use the same confidence map technique to fuse two kinds of cues for robust estimation of the shape of rooms.

Wall segments in landmark models: These wall segments are not only part of the external boundary of the hallway but also the boundary of the room. Therefore, the places inside the detected wall segments are part of the room with high confidence.

Motion traces inside the room: We have a data-gathering micro-task similar to CWC to collect data for rooms. A user takes a photo of a landmark, and then walks into this room. After walking for a while, the user exits and takes another photo. The photos are used to determine the initial/final locations of the trace, and the area along the trace receives confidence. We perform similar thresholding of the cumulated confidence to determine the accessibility of each cell, producing room reconstruction results similar to that shown in Fig. 2.9h. The final floor plan at the end of map augmentation is in Fig. 2.9i.

2.6 Connection Area Detection

So far, we have generated the floor plan of a single floor. However, typical indoor environments always contain multiple floors, along with connection areas between adjacent floors (e.g., stairs, elevators, and escalators). We find that the inertial and wireless signals (e.g., WiFi and cellular) have distinctive patterns when a user passes through such areas. We use unsupervised classification to detect such patterns without training process and develop refinement algorithm to correct detection errors.

2.6.1 Types of Connection Areas

Stairs generate repetitive jolts, hence periodic acceleration fluctuations in the gravity direction when a user climbs. Note that going upstairs or downstairs may cause different jolting patterns, and we need to recognize each of them correctly. We also need to distinguish stairs from walking on the same flat floor. A significant clue is that WiFi signatures always change dramatically between two different floors. We use *WiFi cosine distance* [27], i.e., the cosine value of the angle between two vectors of WiFi signatures, to represent their similarity. Higher cosine distance indicates similar WiFi signatures, and vice versa. From large amounts of experiment data, we observe that WiFi cosine distance between stairs is mostly between $0.65 \sim 0.75$, apparently lower than that of walking on the same floor ($0.8 \sim 0.85$).

Inertial patterns are also differentiated between walking on floor and stairs. Figure 2.10 indicates that the acceleration correlation between heading direction and gravity direction is much lower on the floor than that of stairs. Figure 2.11 shows the acceleration along gravity direction is much lower for upstairs than downstairs: the reason is that gravity is impeding/helping user motion when walking up/down stairs.

Escalators and elevators. Users always stand still in elevators/escalator while their absolute positions change dramatically. To distinguish from standing on the floor, we observe that the WiFi cosine distance between beginning and end of escalator/elevator rides are always significantly smaller ($0.65 \sim 0.8$), compared to standing on the ground for a similar duration (~ 0.95). This observation can be used to distinguish them from standing on the floor. Furthermore, elevators can be easily detected via obvious fading of cellular signals (more than 30 dbm based on our measurements).

To tell the moving direction (up or down), we observe that there are temporary decrease and increase of acceleration along gravity direction at the beginning/end of the ride (Fig. 2.12), and the opposite for going up. We compute the difference of 5 s time window average for the beginning/end of the ride to detect the direction.

Fig. 2.10 Acceleration correlation between heading and gravity directions

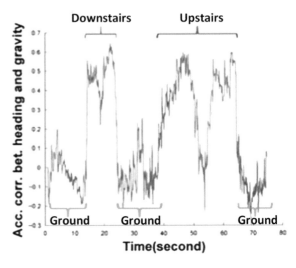

Fig. 2.11 Acceleration along gravity direction

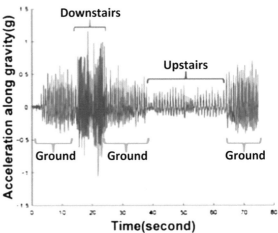

Fig. 2.12 Acceleration along gravity direction for downward escalator/elevator, after Butterworth filter

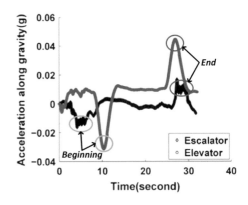

2.6.2 Features

We extract the following features from inertial, WiFi, and cellular data for recognizing the type of connection area:

(1) **Acc MNAC** and **Acc STD**: Acc MNAC denotes the maximum normalized autocorrelation of acceleration along gravity direction, which computes the period of repetitive walking patterns; Acc STD is the standard deviation of that acceleration, which implies user movements. They have been used to tell whether a user is standing still or walking [8].

(2) **Acc COR** and **Acc PV**: Acc COR is the acceleration correlation between heading and gravity directions; it helps to identify stairs; Acc PV are peak values of acceleration along gravity direction; they are used to distinguish their up/down cases [14].

(3) **WiFi CD**: WiFi cosine distance between two endpoints of a time window. This feature tells whether a user passes through floors. The intuition is that WiFi cosine distance between two floors is obviously smaller than staying on the same floor for a short time window (e.g., $\sim$15 s of passing across adjacent floors).

(4) **Cellular SD**: Cellular signal declination. This feature helps to identify the elevator since the closed metal environment dramatically attenuates signals.

2.6.3 Unsupervised Classification

Next, we propose an unsupervised classification algorithm to identify different types of connection areas. We avoid learning techniques that require training that is difficult in practice, especially for crowdsourced mobile users, and training models in various environments always differ a lot. Instead, we automatically cluster the features into different categories and develop an unsupervised classification algorithm via majority voting.

Step 1: Walking detection. Zee [8] computes walking periods on each trace but it relies on hard thresholds of Acc MNAC and Acc STD. We observe that those thresholds change dramatically for different user walking styles and different smartphones, which makes uniform settings impossible. We propose a pre-task in data collection: before walking a CWC micro-task, a user stands still for around 5 s, and then walks with the phone held steady. We leverage k-means algorithm [28] ($k = 2$) to generate the thresholds for each user and obtain similar results in [8] with step counting errors only at start/end of a trace.

Step 2-1: Stairs detection: if a user is walking, we identify whether he/she walks on the floor or stairs. We set the time window as 15 s (approximate time for walking to an adjacent floor via stairs), leverage Acc COR and WiFi CD features, and use the k-means algorithm for recognition (with $k = 2$ for ground/stairs). For stairs, we use Acc PV feature and k-means to identify the up/down direction.

Step 2-2: Escalator/elevator detection: if a user is standing still, we identify whether it is an escalator/elevator or the floor. We compute WiFi CD and cellular SD features for the whole standing still period and use k-means to identify each of them (with $k = 3$ for escalator/elevator/ground). To detect up/down, we compare the average acceleration along gravity direction at the start/end of the ride, i.e., larger at the end than the start of the ride when going down, and vice versa. The above detection achieves very high accuracy (close to 100%).

2.6.4 Refinement and Placement

While most of the above detection results are found to be correct, we observe that occasional errors can happen (e.g., a CWC data on the ground is incorrectly recognized as passing stairs, or an upward escalator is detected as downward). We use a simple majority voting to correct those minority errors.

We abstract a connection graph where nodes are landmarks, and each CRC/CWC constraint forms an edge between two landmarks, with a weight for its constraint type. Multiple edges may exist between two nodes when different constraints were measured. To correct erroneous edges, we use majority voting from all edges between two nodes to decide their connection relation (e.g., on the same story, upward or downward) and remove incorrect detections (Fig. 2.13).

2.6.5 Types of Connection Areas

We also need to generate locations of different types of connection areas on the reconstructed floor plan. For stairs, we place them via the 90-degree turn at its

Fig. 2.13 Landmark connection edges of an elevator between two floors. Majority voting is used to correct detection errors

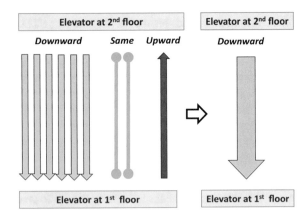

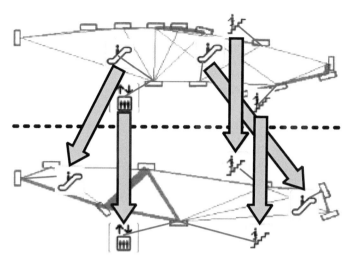

Fig. 2.14 Landmark connection graph of two floors. Line segments represent landmark connection on the same floor, with width for inputs quantity; arrows represent downward connections

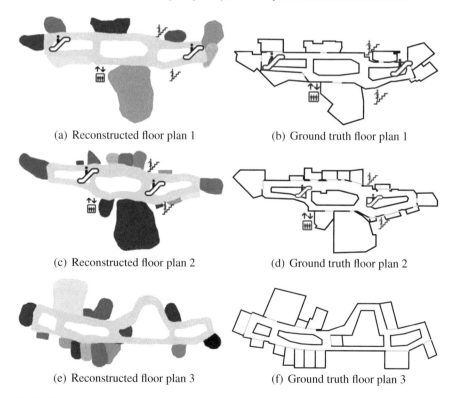

(a) Reconstructed floor plan 1   (b) Ground truth floor plan 1

(c) Reconstructed floor plan 2   (d) Ground truth floor plan 2

(e) Reconstructed floor plan 3   (f) Ground truth floor plan 3

Fig. 2.15 Reconstructed floor plans and ground truth floor plans

start/end points; for escalator and elevator, they are placed via user standing still locations on traces.

The final connection graph for mall 1 is shown in Fig. 2.14, which shows 100% correct detection of four types of landmark connection relations: the same floor, stairs, escalator, and elevator connection. The floor plans with connection areas are shown in Fig. 2.15a and c.

2.7 Performance

We conduct experiments in three environments: two stories of a 150×75 m shopping mall (labeled story 1 and 2) of irregular shape, and one story of a 140×40 m long and narrow mall comprised of two parts connected by two long corridors (labeled part I and II of story 3). In these environments, we select 8, 13, and 14 store entrances as landmarks and collect about 150 photos at different distances and angles for each landmark. In each environment, we have 182, 184, and 151 locations where users conduct "Click-Rotate-Click" (CRC) to take two images of two nearby landmarks, and 24 "Click-Walk-Click" (CWC) to take two images of two far away landmarks in different parts in story 3. We also collect 96, 106, and 73 user traces along the hallway of each environment, and about seven traces inside each store. To connect two stories of the first shopping mall, we observe that there are two stairs, two escalators, and one elevator connecting them. Thus, we also conduct 40 CWC measurements between two stories passing up/down for each stair, and 14 CWC measurements passing up/down for each escalator and elevator.

During data collection, users follow simple guidelines: (1) choose landmarks as large physical objects on the wall, such as store entrances and posters; (2) during walking, hold the phone steady; (3) take photos with the landmark in the center, and without obstructions and moving people on the image. These guidelines help users gather data of higher quality, and user feedbacks suggest the guidelines are easy to follow in practice.

The reconstructed floor plans and their respective ground truths are shown in Fig. 2.15a, c, e and Fig. 2.15b, d, f.

Positions of feature points. We evaluate the quality of floor plans using the root mean square error (RMSE). Given n feature positions on a floor plan with 2D coordinates $X_i^{map} = (x_i^{map}, y_i^{map})$, and their corresponding ground truth coordinates $X_i^{test} = (x_i^{test}, y_i^{test})$, $i = 1, 2, ..., n$, the RMSE is calculated by

$$e_{RMS} = \sqrt{\frac{\sum_{i=1}^{n} (X_i^{map} - X_i^{test})^2}{n}}. \tag{2.10}$$

For each environment, we select two sets of feature positions: one for landmarks and the other for center points of hallway intersections. We can see that RMSEs of landmarks are small (e.g., <1.5 m) while those for intersections are slightly larger.

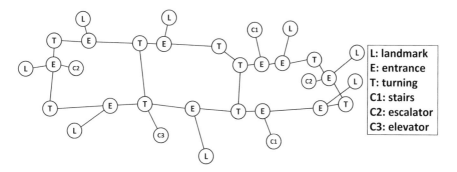

Fig. 2.16 Topological map of reconstructed floor plan for story 1, where nodes "L" denote rooms of landmarks, nodes "E" denote entrances along hallway, nodes "T" denote turnings along hallway, and nodes "C1/C2/C3" denote three types of connection areas

Note that for story 3, we calculate the RMSEs for the left and the right part separately since each part was reconstructed using relatively accurate CRC data while the connecting hallway between them uses less precise CWC data.

Hallway shape. We also evaluate how close the shapes of constructed hallways resemble the respective ground truth. We overlay the reconstructed hallway onto its ground truth to achieve maximum overlap by aligning both the center point and the orientation. Precision is the ratio of the size of the overlap area to the whole reconstructed hallway, and recall is that to the ground truth hallway. F-score is the harmonic average of precision and recall. We can see that Jigsaw achieves a precision around 80%, a recall around 90% and an F-score around 84% for the first two stories. This shows the effect of the calibration of traces by camera locations, and probabilistic occupancy maps are more robust to errors and outliers. The reason that recalls are higher than precisions (as shown in Fig. 2.15) is that reconstructed hallway is a little thicker than the ground truth due to errors in traces. Story 3 has a relatively lower performance because only CWC data can be used to connect the left and right parts.

Room size. We use the error of reconstructed room size as the metric. Jigsaw achieves an average error of 25.6%, 28.3% and 28.9%, respectively, for three stories. Given the fact that some part of the room is not accessible, the errors are relatively small since camera localization provides accurate anchor points to calibrate the errors of inertial traces and the probabilistic occupancy map provides robustness to outliers.

Topological structure. For indoor navigation, the topological structure of a floor plan is more important than its shape/size. We use a topological map where nodes are regions and an edge between two nodes denotes the adjacency of corresponding regions. Nodes can be the intersection points of hallways, or between hallways and landmarks. A landmark's room is also a node. Such a topological map can be used to find the navigation route to a given destination.

To evaluate the topology of the reconstructed map, we extract and compare the topological maps from the grid maps for both ground truth and reconstructed floor plans. Figure 2.16 shows the topological maps of the floor plan on story 1 produced by Jigsaw. We observe that its topological structure is the same as that of its ground truth (the same for story 2 and 3).

2.8 Discussion

Photo-taking operations involve more user efforts, and they provide more accurate geometry information of landmarks than inertial data. We have invited more than 30 users to collect data and found that if a user is paid (e.g., ~$20), he is willing to spend a few minutes practicing data collection following simple guidelines. We observe that they do exhibit more attention on gathering both images and inertial data after receiving the rewards, and their feedbacks suggest the guidelines are easy to follow in practice.

We have tried Jigsaw in other types of buildings where the environments are homogeneous, e.g., an office and a lab building. We find that all components in Jigsaw perform well except SfM, because it relies on abundant feature points matching among images. In office and lab, landmarks (e.g., doors on blank walls) have similar appearances and feature points are much less. Thus, SfM could not create the point cloud needed for landmark modeling. If we replace SfM with other techniques that do not rely on feature points, we could still create maps for those building types.

Our landmark model needs image classification so that images of the same landmark are used as input. With proper and sufficient incentives, users may be willing to tag photos to help ease the classification. There also has been study [29] on automated classification that can achieve high accuracy, and the scale-invariant features extracted by SIFT [20] gives robustness against image differences in resolution, orientation, and illumination conditions. Since there might be several landmarks with similar appearances, one future work is to combine image similarity with WiFi signatures and mobile trajectory to identify those landmarks.

Accurate user trajectories are shown quite challenges [8, 21] because inertial data is impacted by many factors such as the make/model, the position of device (e.g., in hand/pocket), the relative movement of human body (e.g., holding still vs. swinging arms). Some of these may change during the user movements. In light of that, we assign a relatively lower confidence to such trajectories and use a probabilistic model when using them to build hallway and room occupancy maps.

The collection of image and inertial data consumes energy. Jigsaw uses downsized images of 800×600 resolution, each about 100 kB. We use Monsoon Power Monitor [30] (a standard tool for power measurement on a mobile device) to measure the energy cost of micro-tasks. Taking the largest micro-task in our experiments as an example, which consists of two photos taken at the start/end of 2 min walking, it costs around 174 J. Based on WiFi radio transmission power of 720 mW and practical speed of 700 kB/s [31], uploading all data (~780 kB) in this micro-task costs 0.8 J. Compared to the battery capacity of 19 kJ [32], the largest micro-task constitutes a mere 0.92% energy consumption.

2.9   Related Work

Floor plan construction. Indoor floor plan construction is a relatively new problem in mobile computing. A few pieces of work has conducted very valuable initial investigation, using mostly inertial and WiFi data. CrowdInside [14] leverages inertial data from accelerometer, gyroscope, and compass to reconstruct users' mobile trajectories, and use "anchor points" with unique sensing data such as stairs and locations with GPS reception to correct accumulated errors. The trajectories serve as hints about accessible areas, from which hallways, rooms can be identified. Such "anchor" points are also used for user localization (e.g., Unloc [7]). Compared to it, we combine vision and mobile techniques of complementary strengths, extracting detailed geometry information about individual landmarks from images, while inferring the structure and shapes of the hallway and rooms from inertial data. We also use optimization and probabilistic techniques so that the results are robust to errors and outliers in crowdsensed data.

MapGenie [13] uses mobile trajectories as well but it leverages foot-mounted IMU (inertial measurement unit) which is less affected by different positions of the phone, while we use smartphones which are more suitable for crowdsensing. Walkie-Markie [11] leverages WiFi signals, and it uses locations where the trend of WiFi signal strength reverses direction as anchor points, which are found to be more stable than signatures themselves. However, it only constructs the rough hallway skeleton while we also construct both hallways and rooms with accurate geometry and shape. SmartSLAM [12] utilizes WiFi signals and applies dynamic Bayesian network on the smartphones, and it also focuses on just hallway skeleton instead of complete floor plans. Jiang et al. [10] propose a series of algorithms to detect similarities in WiFi signatures between different rooms and hallway segments to find their adjacency, and combine inertial data to obtain hallway lengths and orientations to construct floor plans. However, they manually associate WiFi fingerprints with each room ID, and assume regular building layouts (e.g., hallways with straight segments and right turns, rooms are adjoined and in rectangle shapes), while we automatically cluster landmarks without any manual intervention, and our occupancy grid map technique is robust to arbitrary building layouts.

SLAM. Learning maps in an unexplored environment are the famous SLAM (simultaneous localization and mapping) problem in robotics [33]. One has to estimate the poses (2D/3D locations and orientations) of the robot and locations of landmarks from robot control and environment measurement parameters. Various sensors such as odometry, depth/stereo cameras, and laser rangers are used.

We share similar goals with SLAM, but our input and problem have significant differences. First, crowdsensed data is not just noisy, but also piecewise, collected from mostly uncoordinated users. While in SLAM, a robot usually has special high-precision sensors (e.g., laser ranges, depth/stereo cameras) and systematically explores all accessible areas. We use commodity mobile devices which do not have such sensors; the mobile trajectories are also highly noisy due to error accumulation. Second, we estimate landmarks' orientations as well, while SLAM does only their locations. The existence of loops in the dependence relationship of measurements also adds to the complexity of our problem.

3D construction. There has been a significant amount of literature for reconstructing the 3D model of buildings in computer vision. They take different approaches and require different kinds and amount of data. Some use laser ranger data to produce very detailed and accurate exterior models [34]. Indoor floor plan is essentially a 2D model and we realize that indiscriminate and uniform details are not necessary. This insight enables us to use vision techniques for individual landmarks only while using much lighter weight mobile techniques for landmark placement, hallway, and rooms. This approach greatly reduces the effort and overhead for capturing and processing a large amount of data (some of which may require special hardware such as laser rangers not available on commodity mobile devices), yet still generates reasonably complete and accurate floor plans.

Indoor localization. LiFS [9] leverages the user motion to construct the signature map and crowdsources its calibration to users. Zee [8] tracks inertial sensors in mobile devices carried by users while simultaneously performing WiFi scans. Multidimensional scaling technique [35] is also used to locate WiFi APs from radio scans, so as to build a positioning system without the floor plan. These admirable work produce the signature map, while we construct the floor plan with geometry and shape/sizes of indoor elements such as hallways and rooms. Furthermore, our reconstructed floor plans can be used as constraints to improve localization accuracy (as used in Zee [8] and VeTrack [36]).

Computer vision techniques have been used for localization as well. Sextant [37] leverages photos and gyroscope on smartphones to measure users' relative positions to physical objects, thus localizing users. We simply leverage the ability of SfM to compute the pose, thus the location of the camera taking the image.

2.10   Conclusion

In this chapter, we propose Jigsaw, which combines vision and mobile techniques that take crowdsensed images and inertial data to produce multistory floor plans for complex indoor environments. It addresses one fundamental obstacle to the ubiquitous coverage of indoor localization service: lack of floor plans at service providers. Jigsaw enables service providers to reconstruct floor plans at scale from mobile users' data, thus avoiding the intensive efforts and time needed in business negotiations or environment surveys. We have presented the detailed design and conducted extensive experiments in three stories (two with irregular shapes) of two large shopping malls. The results demonstrate that Jigsaw can produce complete and accurate locations/orientations of landmarks, and structures/shapes of hallways, rooms, and connection areas.

References

1. N.E. Klepeis, W.C. Nelson, W.R. Ott, J.P. Robinson, A.M. Tsang, P. Switzer, J.V. Behar, S.C. Hern, W.H. Engelmann et al., The national human activity pattern survey (nhaps): a resource for assessing exposure to environmental pollutants. J. Expo. Anal. Environ. Epidemiol. **11**(3), 231–252 (2001)
2. H. Surmann, A. Nüchter, J. Hertzberg, An autonomous mobile robot with a 3d laser range finder for 3d exploration and digitalization of indoor environments. Robot. Auton. Syst. **45**(3), 181–198 (2003)
3. K. Khoshelham, S.O. Elberink, Accuracy and resolution of kinect depth data for indoor mapping applications. Sensors **12**(2), 1437–1454 (2012)
4. J.D. Tardós, J. Neira, P.M. Newman, J.J. Leonard, Robust mapping and localization in indoor environments using sonar data. Int. J. Robot. Res. **21**(4), 311–330 (2002)
5. R. Gao, M. Zhao, T. Ye, F. Ye, Y. Wang, K. Bian, T. Wang, X. Li, Jigsaw: indoor floor plan reconstruction via mobile crowdsensing, in *ACM MobiCom* (2014), pp. 249–260
6. R. Ganti, F. Ye, H. Lei, Mobile crowdsensing: current state and future challenges, in *IEEE Communication Magzine* (2011), pp. 32–39
7. H. Wang, S. Sen, A. Elgohary, M. Farid, M. Youssef, R.R. Choudhury, No need to war-drive: unsupervised indoor localization, in *ACM MobiSys* (2012), pp. 197–210
8. A. Rai, K.K. Chintalapudi, V.N. Padmanabhan, R. Sen, Zee: zero-effort crowdsourcing for indoor localization, in *ACM MobiCom* (2012), pp. 293–304
9. Z. Yang, C. Wu, Y. Liu, Locating in fingerprint space: wireless indoor localization with little human intervention, in *ACM MobiCom* (2012), pp. 269–280
10. Y. Jiang, Y. Xiang, X. Pan, K. Li, Q. Lv, R. P. Dick, L. Shang, M. Hannigan, Hallway based automatic indoor floorplan construction using room fingerprints, in *ACM UbiComp* (2013), pp. 315–324
11. G. Shen, Z. Chen, P. Zhang, T. Moscibroda, Y. Zhang, Walkie-markie: indoor pathway mapping made easy, in *NSDI* (2013), pp. 85–98
12. H. Shin, Y. Chon, H. Cha, Unsupervised construction of an indoor floor plan using a smartphone. IEEE Trans. Syst. Man Cybern. **42**(6), 889–898 (2012)
13. D. Philipp, P. Baier, C. Dibak, F. Drr, K. Rothermel, S. Becker, M. Peter, D. Fritsch, Mapgenie: grammar-enhanced indoor map construction from crowd-sourced data, in *PerCom* (2014), pp. 139–147
14. M. Alzantot, M. Youssef, Crowdinside: automatic construction of indoor floorplans, in *SIGSPATIAL* (2012), pp. 99–108
15. Gigwalk, http://www.gigwalk.com
16. Zaarly, https://www.zaarly.com
17. D. Yang, G. Xue, X. Fang, J. Tang, Crowdsourcing to smartphones: incentive mechanism design for mobile phone sensing, in *ACM MobiCom* (2012), pp. 173–184
18. N. Snavely, I. Simon, M. Goesele, R. Szeliski, M. Seitzs, Scene reconstruction and visualization from community photo collections. Proc. IEEE **98**(8), 1370–1390 (2010)
19. D.C. Lee, M. Hebert, T. Kanade, Geometric reasoning for single image structure recovery, in *IEEE CVPR* (2009), pp. 2136–2143
20. D.G. Lowe, Object recognition from local scale-invariant features, in *IEEE ICCV* (1999), pp. 1150–1157
21. N. Roy, H. Wang, R.R. Choudhury, I am a smartphone and i can tell my users walking direction, in *ACM MobiSys* (2014), pp. 329–342
22. F. Dellaert, M. Kaess, Square root sam: simultaneous localization and mapping via square root information smoothing. Int. J. Robot. Res. **25**(12), 1181–1203 (2006)
23. S. Huang, Y. Lai, U. Frese, G. Dissanayake, How far is slam from a linear least squares problem? in *Intelligent Robots and Systems (IROS)* (2010), pp. 3011–3016
24. H.W. Kuhn, The hungarian method for the assignment problem. Naval Res. Logist. Q. **2**(1–2), 83–97 (1955)

25. S. Thrun, Learning occupancy grid maps with forward sensor models. Auton. Robots **15**(2), 111–127 (2003)
26. N. Otsu, A threshold selection method from gray-level histograms. IEEE Trans. Syst. Man Cybern. **9**(1), 62–66 (1979)
27. Cosine distance, https://en.wikipedia.org/wiki/Cosine_similarity
28. K-means clustering, https://en.wikipedia.org/wiki/K-means_clustering
29. S. Wang, J. Joo, Y. Wang, S.C. Zhu, Weakly supervised learning for attribute localization in outdoor scenes, in *IEEE CVPR* (2013), pp. 3111–3118
30. Monsoon power monitor, https://www.msoon.com/LabEquipment/PowerMonitor
31. A. Carroll, G. Heiser, An analysis of power consumption in a smartphone, in *USENIX ATC* (2010), pp. 21–34
32. iphone 4s spec, https://en.wikipedia.org/wiki/IPhone_4S
33. H. Durrant-Whyte, T. Bailey, Simultaneous localisation and mapping (slam): part I the essential algorithms. IEEE Robot. Autom. Mag. **13**(2), 99–110 (2006)
34. C.A. Vanegas, D. Aliaga, B. Benes, Automatic extraction of manhattan-world building masses from 3d laser range scans. IEEE Trans. Visual Comput. Graphics **18**(10), 1627–1637 (2012)
35. J. Koo, H. Cha, Autonomous construction of a wifi access point map using multidimensional scaling, in *PerCom* (2011), pp. 115–132
36. M. Zhao, T. Ye, R. Gao, F. Ye, Y. Wang, G. Luo, Vetrack: real time vehicle tracking in unin-strumented indoor environments, in *ACM SenSys* (2015), pp. 99–112
37. Y. Tian, R. Gao, K. Bian, F. Ye, T. Wang, Y. Wang, X. Li, Towards ubiquitous indoor localization service leveraging environmental physical features, in *IEEE INFOCOM* (2014), pp. 55–63

Chapter 3
Incremental Indoor Map Construction with a Single User

Abstract Lacking of floor plans is a fundamental obstacle to ubiquitous indoor location-based services. Recent work have made significant progress to accuracy, but they largely rely on slow crowdsensing that may take weeks or even months to collect enough data. In this chapter, we propose Knitter that can generate accurate floor maps by a single random user's one-hour data collection efforts, and demonstrate how such maps can be used for indoor navigation. Knitter extracts high-quality floor layout information from single images, calibrates user trajectories, and filters outliers. It uses a multi-hypothesis map fusion framework that updates landmark positions/orientations and accessible areas incrementally according to evidences from each measurement. Our experiments on three different large buildings and 30+ users show that Knitter produces correct map topology, and 90-percentile landmark location and orientation errors of $3 \sim 5$ m and $4 \sim 6°$, comparable to the state of the art at more than $20\times$ speed up: data collection can finish in about one hour even by a novice user trained just a few minutes.

3.1 Introduction

Lacking of floor plans is a fundamental obstacle to ubiquitous location-based services indoors. Recently, some academic work have made admirable progress to automatic floor plan construction. They require only commodity mobile devices (e.g., smartphones) thus scalable construction can be achieved by crowdsensing data from many common users. Among others [1–6], CrowdInside [7] uses mobility traces to derive the approximate shapes of accessible areas; realizing that inertial and WiFi data are inherently noisy thus difficult to produce precise and detailed maps, a recent work Jigsaw [8] further includes images to generate highly accurate floor plans.

Despite such progress, these approaches usually require large amounts of data, crowdsensed from many random users piece by piece, resulting in long data collection time (weeks or even months) before maps can be constructed. In this chapter, we propose *Knitter*, which can construct complete, accurate floor plans within hours. Even in large complex environments such as shopping malls, the data collection for a level takes only about one man-hour's effort. Instead of crowdsensing the data from

© The Author(s) 2018
R. Gao et al., *Smartphone-Based Indoor Map Construction*,
SpringerBriefs in Computer Science, https://doi.org/10.1007/978-981-10-8378-5_3

many random users, Knitter requires only one user to walk along a loop path inside the building to collect small amounts of measurement data. Knitter is highly resilient to low user skill and thus data quality: with just a few minutes' practice, a novice user can collect data that produce maps at quality on par to well-trained users.

The greatly improved speed and resilience using sparse and noisy data are made possible by several novel techniques. A single image localization method extracts high-quality relative spatial relationship and geometry attributes of indoor places of interests (POIs, such as store entrances in shopping malls, henceforth called *landmarks*). This greatly reduces the amount of data needed. Image-aided calibration and optimization-based cleaning methods correct noises in user trajectories, and align them on a common plane. Thus, outliers causing significant skews are identified and filtered. Instead of making a single and final "best" guess of map layout [8], which becomes accurate only after large amounts of data, Knitter takes *multi-hypothesis* measurements. It accumulates measurement evidences upon each data sample, updates parallel possibilities of map layouts incrementally, and chooses those supported by the strongest evidences. Collectively, these techniques enable Knitter to produce complete and accurate maps using sparse and noisy data from novice users. We then demonstrate how such maps can be used to help users navigate and reach particular destinations indoors. Specifically, we make the following contributions:

- We develop a novel localization method that can extract the user's relative distance and orientation to a landmark using a single image, and produce multiple hypotheses about the landmark's geometry attributes.
- We devise image-aided angle and stride length calibration methods to reduce errors in user trajectories, and optimization-based discrepancy minimization to align multiple trajectories along the same loop path, thus detecting and filtering outliers.
- We propose an incremental floor plan construction framework based on dynamic Bayesian networks, and design algorithms that update parallel map layout possibilities using evidences from measurement data, while tolerating inevitable residual noises and errors.
- We devise a landmark recognition algorithm that combines complementary data to determine measurement/landmark correspondence, methods for accessible area confidence assignment under sparse data, and a topology-based navigation approach that gives turn-by-turn instructions to users to reach indoor destinations, none fully addressed in previous work.
- We develop a prototype and conduct extensive experiments in three kinds of large (up to $140 \times 50\,\text{m}^2$), typical indoor environments: featureless offices and labs, and feature-rich shopping malls, with 30+ users. We find that Knitter achieves accuracy comparable to the state of the art [8] (e.g., 90-percentile position/orientation errors at $3 \sim 5\,\text{m}$ and $4 \sim 6°$), with more than $20\times$ speed up that costs only one hour's efforts of a single user, and the reconstructed map can be used directly for localization.

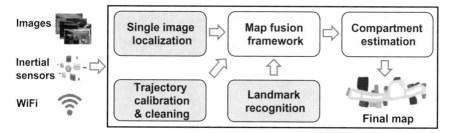

Fig. 3.1 Knitter contains several components to produce complete and accurate maps by a single random user's one hour data collection efforts

3.2 Overview

Knitter takes several components in system measurements, map fusion framework, and compartment estimation to produce the final map (shown in Fig. 3.1).

Three system measurement techniques are devised to produce inputs to the map fusion framework from sensing data: (1) *single-image localization* extracts a landmark's geometry information, including its relative orientation, distance to the user, and its adjacent wall segment lengths from one image; (2) *trajectory calibration* leverages the image localization results to reduce user trajectory angle and stride length errors, and then *trajectory cleaning* quantifies the trajectory quality and uses alignment and clustering to detect and filter outliers; (3) *landmark recognition* combines image, inertial and WiFi data of complementary strengths to determine which measurement data corresponds to which landmark, thus ensuring correct map update. The *map fusion framework* fuses previous measurement results to create maps under a dynamic Bayesian network formulation. It represents multiple possible map layouts each with different estimations of landmark positions as hidden states, represented by random variables, infers, and updates their probability distributions incrementally, using evidences upon each additional measurement. The *compartment estimation* combines evidences from different kinds of measurements to properly assign accessible confidences to cells in an occupancy grid, such that estimations of compartment (e.g., hallways, rooms) shapes and sizes are accurate even with small amount of data.

3.3 Localization via a Single Image

Single image localization estimates the relative distance d and orientation θ of the user to a landmark in photo (shown in Fig. 3.2). It also produces multiple hypotheses of the landmark's geometry attributes, with a weight (probability) for each hypothesis' measurement confidence. Such output is fed to the map fusion framework. Unlike most vision-based localization work [9] that relies on image matching to a database of known landmarks, we use line extraction and do not need any prior benchmark images.

Fig. 3.2 Landmark's
geometry layout

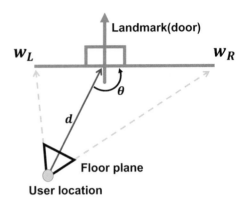

Preprocessing. First, we use Canny edge detector [10] to extract line segments
(Fig. 3.4c) from an image (Fig. 3.4a). We cluster them [11] and find the vanishing
point (VP) where the wall/ground boundary line and horizon line intersect, and obtain
its pixel coordinates (u, v).

Estimating θ. Based on projective geometry, we can compute the relative orientation
angle θ of the landmark to the camera using the vanishing point's coordinates:

$$\theta = \pi - mod(\arctan(\frac{u - \frac{W}{2}}{f}), \pi),\tag{3.1}$$

where W is the image width in pixels and f is the camera's focal length in pixels
computed from the camera's parameter specifications.

Estimating d. Assuming the user points, the camera downwards (or upwards) at an
angle α (shown in Fig. 3.3), d can be computed as follows:

$$\tan \alpha = \frac{h_0}{f}, \tan \beta = \frac{h_b}{f}, d = h_u \cdot \cot(\alpha + \beta),\tag{3.2}$$

Fig. 3.3 Estimation of
distance d

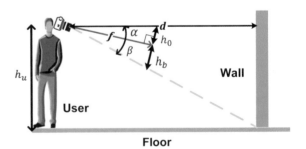

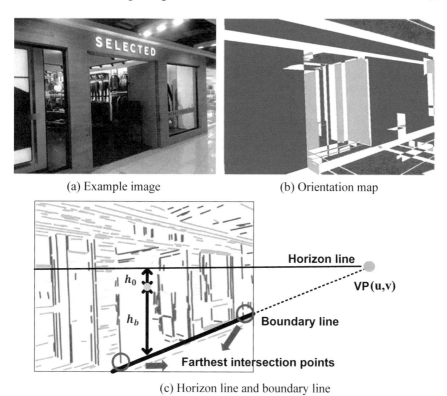

(a) Example image   (b) Orientation map

(c) Horizon line and boundary line

Fig. 3.4 Extracted horizon line and boundary line on the example image (better viewed in color). Red circles denote farthest intersection points between vertical line segments and boundary line

where h_0 denotes the vertical distance of the horizon line to the image center, derivable from (u, v), h_b the vertical distance from the image center to the boundary line (both marked in Fig. 3.4c), and h_u is the actual camera height which can be approximated using the user's height (input by the user or estimated).

Computing h_b in Eq. 3.2 requires us to identify the floor–wall boundary line (Fig. 3.4c). This is not straightforward because there may exist many other lines that are parallel to the true boundary. Reliably distinguishing them from the real one is difficult. We develop two methods to produce *multiple hypotheses* of floor–wall boundary so the correct one is included with high probability.

Method 1: intersection counting. After careful observation, we find that the boundary line is usually quite long and has many intersections with vertical line segments (e.g., points denoted in circles in Fig. 3.4c), far more than other parallel lines. We compute a weight w_{l_i} for each candidate line l_i as

$$w_{l_i} = \frac{N_{l_i} \cdot L_{l_i}}{|d_{l_i} - \tilde{d}|}, \tag{3.3}$$

where N_{l_i} denotes the number of intersection points between l_i and vertical line segments, L_{l_i} the length of l_i, d_{l_i} is the photo-taking distance estimated using l_i, and $\tilde{d}$ is the recommended distance (to be elaborated in Sect. 5.6). The numerator indicates how strong a candidate line is, and the denominator filters out incorrect guesses with large deviations to the guideline of medium photo-taking distances. The weights are then normalized to become probabilities.

Method 2: orientation map. We first generate an orientation map [12] (Fig. 3.4b) where the orientation of each surface is computed and its pixels colored accordingly. Given a floor–wall boundary candidate l_i, we compute the fraction of wall and floor pixels with consistent orientations as the weight

$$w_{l_i} = \frac{S_{floor}^+ + S_{wall}^+}{S_{floor}^{all} + S_{wall}^{all}}, \tag{3.4}$$

where S_{floor}^+ and S_{wall}^+ denote the floor/wall pixel areas whose orientations conforming to l_i (i.e., above l_i are walls facing sidewards and below l_i are floors facing upwards), S_{floor}^{all}, and S_{wall}^{all} the respective total pixel areas. The correct candidate should have the best consistency, thus greatest weight.

Estimating (w_L, w_R). Along a boundary line, we detect intersection points with vertical line segments. The left- and right-farthest intersection points are identified in Fig. 3.4c, and their horizontal pixel distances (w_L^p, w_R^p) to the image center are transformed into left and right wall segment lengths (w_L, w_R) based on projective geometry:

$$w_{L,R} = \frac{d \cdot \sin(\arctan(\frac{w_{L,R}^p}{f}))}{\sin(\theta \mp \arctan(\frac{w_{L,R}^p}{f}))} \tag{3.5}$$

Now we have multiple hypotheses, each having a boundary line, user distance/angle, and two wall segment lengths, with a weight (probability). Detailed evaluations (Sect. 5.6) show that this localization method generates quite small errors (<1 m) even at remote distances (>10 m).

3.4   Trajectory Calibration and Cleaning

Accurate user trajectories from inertial data are critical in floor plan construction. In Knitter, the user walks along a closed-loop path multiple times, taking landmark photos and collecting inertial data. Each loop may take about 10 min. Significant errors may accumulate during the long walk, and frequent stops to take landmark photos may create severe inertial disturbances, both resulting in deformed, inaccurate trajectories. We must be able to rectify such errors.

3.4.1 Trajectory Calibration

We tested two trajectory construction methods: a gyroscope-based (Zee [13] and UnLoc [14]) and a recent phone attitude one (A^3 [15]). Although the step counts are relatively accurate, neither of the reference methods produces satisfactory trajectories due to walking direction errors. Figure 3.5b and c show their results for a 5-min walk (Fig. 3.5a). The main reasons are: (1) the gyroscope has significant drifts over long walking periods; (2) during long, straight walk, there are few calibration opportunities of similar changes in compass and gyroscope as required in A^3 [15]; (3) strong electromagnetic disturbances (e.g., server rooms [16]) can cause false "calibrations." We propose image aided methods to calibrate the angles and stride lengths, thus accurate walking direction and trajectories (Fig. 3.5d).

Image-aided Angle Calibration. We leverage "closed loops" to estimate an average gyroscope drift rate δ. After finishing a loop, the user returns to the starting area and takes a second photo of the first landmark. Using single image localization, we compute two angles θ_1, θ_2 based on Eq. 3.1 for both images of that landmark. Their difference $\Delta\theta = \theta_1 - \theta_2$ is the orientation angle change. Since the user may not return perfectly to the starting point, this will cause an additional change in user orientation, which can be measured by the difference of the gyroscope's "yaw" between the two images, denoted as Δg. The rate δ and calibrated angle g_t^* are computed as follows:

$$\delta = \frac{\Delta g + \Delta\theta}{T}, g_t^* = g_t + \delta \cdot t, \tag{3.6}$$

where T is the time between taking the two images. We find this method is not affected by electromagnetic disturbances; it always achieves accurate and robust angle calibration ($\sim 5°$ errors at 90-percentile).

Image-aided Stride Length Calibration. We leverage the closed loop to calibrate the stride length that may change in different regions, e.g., larger in wide and open hallways [7]. Our localization method can compute the user's relative location to the first landmark, thus the location change before and after the loop can be computed as a vector $\mathbf{v}$ pointing from the start to the end location. We compensate each point at time t on the trajectory with $\mathbf{v} \cdot t/T$ to calibrate stride length errors. Figure 3.6

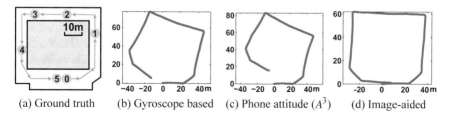

(a) Ground truth   (b) Gyroscope based   (c) Phone attitude (A^3)   (d) Image-aided

Fig. 3.5 Trajectories from **a** ground truth with six photo-takings; **b** gyroscope based [13, 14]; **c** phone attitude [15]; **d** image-aided angle calibration

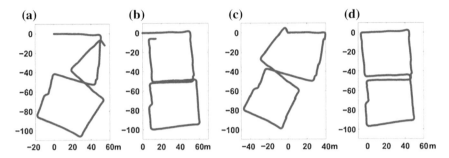

Fig. 3.6 **a** raw trajectory for a closed loop; **b** angle calibration only; **c** stride length calibration only; **d** both calibrations

shows that both angle and stride length calibrations are needed to produce an accurate closed-loop trajectory (Fig. 3.6d).

3.4.2 Trajectory Cleaning

Calibration only rectifies trajectories with small errors, but not outliers. We conduct the following three steps to detect and filter out such outliers: loop screening, loop alignment, and outlier removal.

Loop Screening. We use the "gap", the distance between the starting and ending locations of the angle-calibrated loop for preliminary screening. Since the user returns to the starting area, ideally the gap should be 0 after image compensation. A lower quality loop has a larger gap. Given multiple trajectories, we compute the standard deviation σ of the calibration shift vector's length $|\mathbf{v}|$ normalized over the size of the trajectory, and remove those with $|\mathbf{v}|$ beyond 3σ.[1]

Loop Alignment. Multiple trajectories must be placed within the same global coordinate system. However, the trajectories cannot overlap perfectly with each other. Each time the exact path may differ slightly within the same hallways or isles, so do the stride lengths. Thus, the trajectories have slightly different shapes and possibly scales.

Without loss of generality, we consider how to place a second trajectory with respect to an existing one. Initially, we pick the one with the smallest gap as a reference loop, and use landmark recognition (Sect. 3.6) to detect which landmark c_i on the second loop corresponds to landmark i on the reference loop. This addresses situations where the user takes photos of slightly different sets of landmarks in each loop (due to negligence or imperfect memory). Then, we *translate, rotate, and scale*

---

[1] According to Chebyshev's Theorem, this removes those trajectories with extreme errors beyond 88.9% of all loops.

the second one to achieve "maximum overlap" with the first one, as defined by minimizing the overall pairwise distances of corresponding landmarks:

$$\{\phi^*, O^*, s^*\} = \underset{\phi, O, s}{\operatorname{argmin}} \sum_{i=1}^{N} \|s \cdot R(\phi) \cdot (M_{c_i}^2 - O) - M_i^1\|_2, \qquad (3.7)$$

where $M_i^1 = X_i^1 + Z_i^1$ and $M_{c_i}^2 = X_{c_i}^2 + Z_{c_i}^2$ denote the coordinates of the i_{th} landmark in the reference loop and the corresponding landmark c_i in the second loop, X_i^1 and $X_{c_i}^2$ are the coordinates of photo-taking locations of them, Z_i^1 and $Z_{c_i}^2$ are the relative locations from the user to the landmark (from single image localization). $\{\phi, O, s\}$ denote the rotation, translation, and scale factors to the second trajectory, and $R(\phi) = \begin{bmatrix} \cos\phi & -\sin\phi \\ \sin\phi & \cos\phi \end{bmatrix}$ is the rotation matrix. A simple greedy search for an initial solution followed by iterative perturbation can find the approximate solutions for the three parameters. Each additional trajectory is placed similarly within the common coordinate system.[2]

Outlier Removal. After all trajectories and landmark sets are placed on the same coordinate system, we identify the common subset of s_m landmarks across all loops. We represent those in loop k with a multidimensional vector $(m_{s_1}^k, ..., m_{s_m}^k)$, where $m_{s_i}^k$ is landmark s_i' location, and compute the Euclidean distance between each two vectors. Then, we use a density-based clustering algorithm DBSCAN [17] to eliminate outlier loops: vectors are "reachable" to each other if the distance is within an empirically decided threshold $\varepsilon = 0.8\,\mathrm{m}$, those not reachable from any other vector are detected as outliers, and respective loops are removed.

3.5 Map Fusion Framework

3.5.1 Dynamic Bayesian Network

We use a dynamic Bayesian network framework to fuse the extracted information from previous measurement algorithms to build maps incrementally. It formally represents different states in the floor plan construction process as random variables, and denotes their dependence using arrows (shown in Fig. 3.7). We assume time is slotted. At each time t, x_t denotes the user pose (i.e., camera/phone coordinates and orientation); u_t is the control including the walking distance and heading direction that alter the user pose from x_{t-1} to x_t; z_t is measurement of the landmark by the user (e.g., relative distance d and angle θ); m_{c_t} are the coordinates and orientation of the landmark being measured, $c_t = j$ ($j = 1, ..., N$) is the index of this landmark as detected by landmark recognition (Sect. 3.6).

---

[2] We also tried to place each trajectory w.r.t. all previous ones but find the much increased complexity brought only marginal improvements. Thus, we use the much simpler method as in Eq. 3.7.

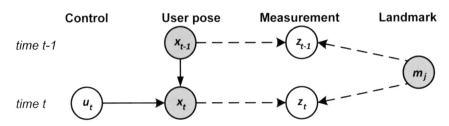

Fig. 3.7 Dynamic Bayesian Network. Gray nodes (user/landmark states) are hidden variables to be computed, and unshaded ones are observation variables measured directly. Arrow directions denote determining relationship, solid for movement update, and dashed for landmark update

In the above, u_t and z_t are *observation variables* that can be measured directly from sensors, while x_t and m_j are *hidden variables* that must be computed from observation ones. These variables are represented by probability distributions. Given control signal $u_{1:t}$ (shorthand for $u_1, ..., u_t$) and measurements $z_{1:t}$, the goal is to compute the posterior (i.e., conditional) probability of both landmark positions $m_{1:N}$ and user poses $x_{1:t}$, i.e., $p(x_{1:t}, m_{1:N}|u_{1:t}, z_{1:t})$.

3.5.2 Particle Filter Algorithm

We use a particle filter algorithm to compute the above user poses and landmark attributes incrementally. We maintain a collection of K "particles." Each particle k ($k = 1, ..., K$) includes a different estimation of:

- user pose x_t: user's coordinates (x, y) and heading direction φ,
- each landmark's mean μ and covariance Σ of its coordinates and orientation (μ_x, μ_y, μ_ϕ), assumed multivariate Gaussian distribution,
- two adjacent wall lengths (w_L, w_R) of each landmark.

At each time slot, we perform five steps to update the states in each particle k.

1. Movement Update: given the previous user pose x_{t-1} at time $t - 1$ and recent control $u_t = (v, \omega)$ where v is the moving speed and ω the heading direction (obtained from trajectory measurement algorithms in Sect. 3.4), the destination is computed by dead reckoning. The current pose x_t is computed by picking a sample from a multivariate Gaussian distribution of many possible locations around the destination (Fig. 3.8):

$$x_t^{[k]} \sim p(x_t|x_{t-1}^{[k]}, u_t) \tag{3.8}$$

2. Landmark Recognition: a new measurement z_t of a nearby landmark m_{c_t} is made at t, and c_t is identified as j ($j \in \{1, ..., N\}$) by the landmark recognition algorithm (to be elaborated in Sect. 3.6). If m_j is never seen before, a new landmark is created, with coordinates and orientation computed based on user pose x_t and relative distance, angle in z_t.

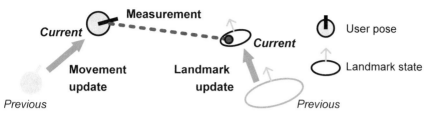

Fig. 3.8 A current user pose is computed based on the previous pose and control signal. Then, a landmark's state is updated using a measurement from the new user pose

3. Landmark Update: If m_j is a known landmark, its states are updated. Assuming the most recent attributes of landmark m_j are μ_j^{t-1} and Σ_j^{t-1}, where $\mu_j^{t-1} = (\mu_x, \mu_y, \mu_\varphi)$ are its coordinates and orientation in the global coordinate system, and Σ_j^{t-1} the corresponding 3×3 covariance matrix.

- *Prediction.* Given a user pose $x_t = (x, y, \varphi)$ at time t and m_j's attributes μ_j^{t-1} at $t-1$, a measurement prediction $\hat{z}_t$ about the relative distance and angle between the user and m_j can be made as

$$\hat{z}_t = \begin{pmatrix} \hat{d} \\ \hat{\theta} \end{pmatrix} = \begin{pmatrix} \sqrt{(\mu_x - x)^2 + (\mu_y - y)^2} \\ \mu_\varphi - \varphi \end{pmatrix} \tag{3.9}$$

simply their differences in coordinates and orientations.
- *Observation.* Given m_j's image, the localization algorithm (Sect. 3.3) generates multiple hypotheses of (d, θ), each with a weight. We pick one hypothesis at probabilities proportional to their weights as the actual measurement $z_t = (d, \theta)^T$.
- *Extended Kalman Filter* (EKF) [18]. It linearizes the measurement model (Eq. 3.9) such that measurement errors become linear functions of noises in user pose and landmark attributes. Then, it computes the "optimal" distribution of hidden variables (e.g., landmark attributes) given observations, such that the discrepancies between predicted and actual measurements are minimized.

Step 1: The Kalman gain is computed as follows:

$$Q = H \Sigma_j^{t-1} H^T + Q_t, \; K = \Sigma_j^{t-1} H^T Q^{-1}, \tag{3.10}$$

where Q_t is a 2×2 covariance of Gaussian measurement noises in (d, θ), H is the 2×3 Jacobian matrix of $\hat{z}_t$, with elements partial derivatives of $(\hat{d}, \hat{\theta})$ w.r.t. $(\mu_x, \mu_y, \mu_\varphi)$.
Step 2: The mean and covariance of m_j are updated as follows:

$$\mu_j^t = \mu_j^{t-1} + K(z_t - \hat{z}_t), \; \Sigma_j^t = (I - KH)\Sigma_j^{t-1} \tag{3.11}$$

where I is a 3×3 unit matrix.

Figure 3.8 shows that after the update, the uncertainties (quantified by covariances represented in oval sizes) in a landmark's location and orientation become less and the distributions become more concentrated. To simplify the wall length estimation, we use an weighted average of $(w_L^{t-1}(t-1) + w_L)/t$ as the updated wall length w_L^t for landmark m_j (w_R computed similarly). We find the results are sufficiently accurate.

4. Weight Update: we assign each particle k a weight that quantifies the probability (Eq. 3.12) that the actual measurement z_t can happen under the user pose $x_t^{[k]}$ and updated landmark states (μ_j^t, Σ_j^t). The larger the probability, the more likely that the estimated user pose and landmark attributes are accurate.

$$
\begin{aligned}
w^{[k]} &= p(z_t | x_t^{[k]}, m_j) \\
&= |2\pi Q|^{-\frac{1}{2}} exp\{-\frac{1}{2}(z_t - \hat{z}_t)^T Q^{-1}(z_t - \hat{z}_t)\}
\end{aligned}
\tag{3.12}
$$

Under Gaussian noises and linearization approximation [19], the weight can be computed in closed form of the actual measurement z_t and its prediction $\hat{z}_t$. A prediction $\hat{z}_t$ closer to actual z_t leads to a larger weight.

5. Resampling: After the weights for all particles are computed, a new set of particles is formed by sampling K particles from the current set, each at probabilities proportional to their weights. The above steps are repeated on the new set for the next time slot.

3.6 Landmark Recognition

Landmark recognition detects which landmark is measured in the current data sample: a new one never seen before, or an existing one already known. Incorrect recognition will cause wrong updates, thus possibly large errors or even incorrect map topology. We take advantage of multiple sensing modalities of complementary strengths for robust recognition: images capture the appearances; poses depict the spatial relationships, and WiFi identifies radio signatures.

Image Based Recognition. Given a test image, we extract its features and compare with those from images of existing landmarks, and then determine whether it is a new or existing one. We use a standard image feature extraction algorithm [20] to generate robust, scale-invariant feature vectors. Then, we identify matched feature vectors to those from an existing landmark's image. The image similarity S_j^{image} to each existing landmark j is computed as the fraction of matching ones among all distinct feature vectors in the test image and landmark j's image.

WiFi-Based Recognition. Although image features distinguish complex landmarks well (e.g., stores and posters), they are ineffective in homogeneous environments such as office and lab, where doors have very similar appearances. We use

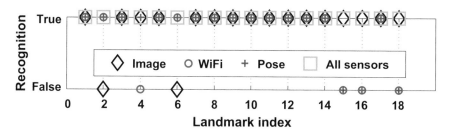

Fig. 3.9 Recognition results for 18 landmarks in the mall during the second loop

the *cosine distance* (i.e., the cosine value of the angle between two vectors of WiFi signatures) to quantify the radio signature similarity S_j^{wifi} between the test data and landmark j's data.

Pose Based Recognition. Given the user pose x_t and landmark attributes (e.g., coordinates and orientation), a relative distance/orientation $\hat{z}_t$ can be predicted from Eq. 3.9. The correct landmark j should make this prediction very close to the actual measurement. Based on this intuition, we use the conditional probability that z_t can occur given x_t and m_j's location/orientation as the metric S_j^{pose}, which is exactly the same as weight $w^{[k]}$ in Eq. 3.12.

Aggregate Similarity. An aggregate similarity is computed as $S_j^{image} \cdot S_j^{wifi} \cdot S_j^{pose}$. Since images, WiFi, and inertial data are independent from each other, the probability the landmark being j is proportional to the product of the three similarity scores. The product form implies that a small score in any of the three is a strong indication of incorrect match, and the true match would have high scores in all the three.

Using the shopping mall in evaluation (Sect. 5.6) as an example, first we collect one loop data as benchmark, and Fig. 3.9 shows the recognition results for 18 landmarks of the second loop. We observe that the recognition using any individual modality can fail: e.g., pose/WiFi for nearby landmarks 15 and 16, and image for glass walls (landmark 2) or similar appearances (landmark 6 to 5). Aggregating them, however, achieves 100% accuracy (more results in Sect. 5.6).

3.7 Compartment Estimation

Besides landmarks, a complete floor plan includes also accessible compartments such as hallways and rooms. A commonly adopted technique is occupancy grid mapping [21]: divide the floor into small cells and accumulate evidence on each cell's accessibility to identify compartments. While existing work [7, 8] uses plenty of trajectories, we have only a handful, too sparse to infer accessible areas directly. We make two adaptations to compensate data sparsity: (1) instead of a fixed confidence in cells, we spread attenuating confidences away from trajectories and detected walls; (2) we leverage regions between the camera and landmarks to infer large open regions.

Hallway and Room Shapes. Since only a few trajectories are gathered, they are too sparse to cover all accessible areas. We assign each cell a confidence that increases as it gets closer to a nearby trace or wall segment, because cells closer to traces or walls are more likely accessible. Areas traversed by multiple traces will accumulate more confidence, thus more likely to be accessible. Figure 3.10a shows two types of hallway boundaries: detected walls have larger probabilities (darker shades) and inferred ones smaller probabilities. One hallway segment is missing because it does not have any landmarks, thus no walls are detected. The missing part is made up from trajectories (Fig. 3.10b). We then use a closed-loop walking inside each room to reconstruct its shape, and leverage landmark recognition to associate such traces with respective rooms and place their contours on the map.

Large Open Regions. Large open regions (e.g., lobbies) need many traces to cover its cells. We leverage the images to infer their sizes. Since the user needs to ensure the landmark is not occluded by obstacles, the region between the camera and the landmark is usually accessible. Thus, we compute the triangle region between the camera and landmark (including adjacent wall segments), and assign a fixed confidence to all cells in this area. Figure 3.10c shows the occupancy grid map with a lobby area filled with dark triangles from additional images, without which there would be a blank hole on Fig. 3.10b.

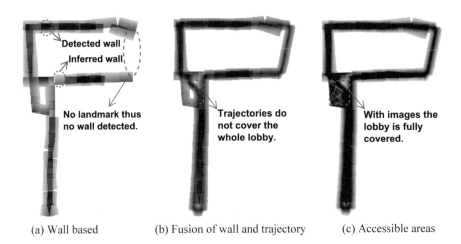

(a) Wall based   (b) Fusion of wall and trajectory   (c) Accessible areas

Fig. 3.10 Combining different evidences for compartment estimation of hallways

3.8 Performance

We define landmarks as store/room entrances, and conduct experiments in three environments: a 90 × 50 m office, a 80 × 50 m lab building and a 140 × 50 m shopping mall, with 16, 24, 18 doors/posters as landmarks, respectively.

We evaluate Knitter's resilience with three user groups: *dedicated users* who are well trained (i.e., ourselves); 15 *novice users* who spend 5 min practicing data collection following two simple guidelines: (1) take images from medium distances and angles (e.g., ∼5 m, ∼45°), with the landmark at the center; (2) during walking, hold the phone steady; and 15 *untrained users* who may not follow the guidelines. Feedback from trained ones suggests that the two guidelines are easy to follow in practice.

The reconstructed maps from five loops' data gathered by novice users and their respective ground truth floor plans are shown in Fig. 3.11. We can see they match the ground truth quite well. To quantify how accurate the shape of a reconstructed map is, we overlay it onto its ground truth to achieve the maximum overlap by rotation and translation. We define precision, recall, and F-score to measure the degree of overlap:

$$P = \frac{S_{re} \cap S_{gt}}{S_{re}}, \ R = \frac{S_{re} \cap S_{gt}}{S_{gt}}, \ F = \frac{2P \cdot R}{P + R}, \tag{3.13}$$

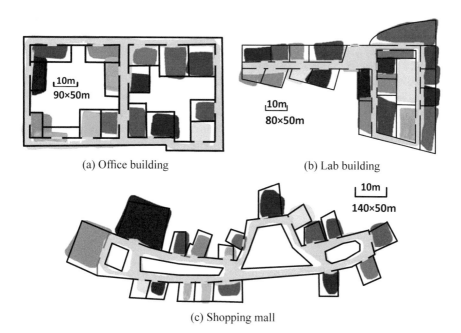

(a) Office building   (b) Lab building

(c) Shopping mall

Fig. 3.11 Reconstructed and ground truth floor plans for the office, lab, and mall

where S_{re} denotes the size of reconstructed map, S_{gt} that of its ground truth, and $S_{re} \cap S_{gt}$ that of the overlapping area.

3.9   Discussion

Incentives for Novice Users. Most existing study [7, 8, 22] reconstruct indoor floor plans via mobile crowdsensing, which assumes casual users who do not pay much attention to data collection. Thus, low-quality data or even errors are common and sifting noises is difficult. We conjecture that with proper amounts and types of incentive, users willing to focus on data collection for short time (e.g., $20 cash reward for 10 minutes) can be recruited. Such novice users can follow simple guidelines and collect data in desired forms and quantities (e.g., landmark images along a loop path). Such a model of task completion using effective rewards has already been validated in the industry [23–26]. Dealing with possible cheating and spam is a practical issue considered in [27].

Robust Landmark Recognition. We combine image, WiFi, and user pose for landmark recognition. Many factors can affect the image matching accuracy: resolution, orientation, distance, illumination (e.g., noon sunlight versus night lights), richness in features (e.g., office versus mall), and occlusions (e.g., objects or people). Thus, we combine WiFi signals and user pose, essentially the measurement location and orientation, for robust recognition. In reality, we find when landmarks are too close (e.g., two adjacent office doors), WiFi and user pose cannot tell them apart. We plan to extend image extraction method to detect multiple landmarks in single image, and leverage magnetic map [28] or fine-grained WiFi propagation models [29] to improve the recognition robustness.

Outlier Trajectories. Accurate user trajectories via inertial data are quite a challenge due to many factors such as the make/model of the phone and thus qualities of embedded sensors, the positions of the device (e.g., in hand/pocket), and relative movements to the human body (e.g., holding still versus swinging) [13–15, 22, 30]. We take advantage of novice users to infer angle and stride length changes for trajectory calibration, and apply cleaning methods to detect and filter outliers. This granularity might be coarse. Useful landmark images and trajectory segments may still exist. We will look into fine-grained outlier filtering so that valuable individual images and trajectory fragments can be identified and used.

Photo-taking for navigation. In our navigation example, users take photos of nearby landmarks to identify the surroundings and pinpoint themselves on the map. In order to reduce user efforts, photos are taken only when necessary, e.g., at the starting point or when users get lost in the building. Wearable devices that can take videos/images automatically (e.g., Google glass) can help alleviate such explicit user efforts. We also plan to leverage WiFi propagation models and magnetic fingerprints for robust landmark recognition and better localization accuracy.

3.10   Related Work

Indoor Floor Plans. Indoor floor maps is a relatively new problem in the mobile community. CrowdInside [7] uses inertial data to construct user trajectories to approximate shapes of accessible areas. Jigsaw [8] combines vision and mobile techniques to generate accurate floor plans using many images. Walkie-Markie [3] identifies when the WiFi signal strength reverses the trend and uses them as calibration points to construct hallways. Jiang et. al. [1] detect room and hallway adjacency from WiFi signature similarity, and combine user trajectories to construct hallways. MapGenie [2] leverages foot-mounted IMU (Inertail Measurement Unit) for more accurate user trajectories. Shin et. al. [4] use mobile trajectories and WiFi signatures in a Bayesian setting for hallway skeletons. Sankar et. al. [31] combine smartphone inertial/video data and manual user recognition to recover room features and model the indoor scene of Manhattan World (i.e., orthogonal walls). IndoorCrowd2D [22] generates panoramic indoor views of Manhattan hallway structures by stitching images together. CrowdMap [32] uses the geometry features such as corners in such panoramic views to create rooms for floor maps.

Compared to them, our distinction is fast, accurate, resilient map construction with a single random user. We produce maps with qualities comparable to the latest method [8], and more than $20\times$ speed up. We also propose incremental map construction utilizing multi-hypothesis inputs and robust landmark recognition, which are suitable for sparse data.

User Trajectories. Accurate user trajectories via inertial data are quite a challenge due to many factors such as the make/model of the phone and thus qualities of embedded sensors, the positions of the device (e.g., in hand/pocket), and relative movements to the human body (e.g., holding still versus swinging). Among others [14, 22, 30, 33], A^3 [15] leverages same changes in compass and gyroscope around turns to identify reliable compass readings and calibrate accumulated errors. Zee [13] combines gyroscope, compass, and an existing map's layout to detect the user's directions and thus trajectories.

In comparison, we need to deal with severe disturbances (e.g., phone rotation, translation during photo-taking, strong electromagnetic sources like machine rooms) and long walking durations (over 10 minutes). On the other hand, we take advantage of freelancer model for images and loop closures to infer angle changes for trajectory calibration, and apply cleaning methods to detect and filter outliers.

Vision-based 3D Reconstruction. Structure from Motion [34] is a famous technique for scene reconstruction. It creates a "point cloud" form of object exterior using large numbers of images from different viewpoints. iMoon [35] and OPS [9] use it for navigation and object positioning. Tango phones from Google [36] use depth cameras to build 3D scenes.

Indoor floor plan is essentially a 2D modeling problem that requires reasonably accurate sizes, shapes of major landmarks, but not uniform details everywhere, which is the strength of 3D reconstruction. Compared to them, our focus is not on vision. We carefully leverage suitable techniques for a novel localization method using a single image, thus deriving landmark geometry attributes. We leverage much lighter weight mobile techniques to process inertial and WiFi data for reasonably accurate floor maps with much less data and complexity.

SLAM (Simultaneous Localization And Mapping) estimates the poses (usually 2D locations and orientations) of the robot and locations of landmarks (mostly feature points on physical objects) in unknown environments. Abundant academic work [37, 38] have leveraged high quality or special sensors such as odometers, depth/stereo cameras, and laser rangers for precise robot motion and landmark measurements. Some recent work [5, 39] have used sensors in commodity mobile devices but mostly focus on localization, not map construction.

Compared to them, we must extract information and create complete maps reliably despite low-quality and quantity data from common users. The precision and variation of sensor data from commodity mobile devices are far worse than those from special hardware in robotics. We also need to filter, fuse fragmented and inconsistent data from random users.

3.11   Conclusion

We propose Knitter, which constructs accurate indoor floor plans requiring only one hour's data collection by a single random user. Compared to the latest work, Knitter creates maps of similar quality with more than $20\times$ speed up, and such maps can be used to provide turn-by-turn indoor navigation instructions. Its speed and resilience come from novel techniques including single image localization, multi-hypothesis input, trajectory calibration, and cleaning methods, and fusion of heterogeneous data's results using an incremental map construction framework that updates map layouts based on measurement evidences. Extensive experiments in three different large indoor environments for 30+ users show that a novice user with a few minutes' training can produce complete and accurate floor plans on par to dedicated users, while incurring only one man-hour's data-gathering efforts.

In the future, we plan to investigate methods to leverage magnetic signatures and WiFi prorogation models to improve landmark recognition accuracy, and filter outlier data at finer granularity to preserve individual images and trajectory fragments of high quality.

References

1. Y. Jiang, Y. Xiang, X. Pan, K. Li, Q. Lv, R.P. Dick, L. Shang, M. Hannigan, Hallway based automatic indoor floorplan construction using room fingerprints, in *ACM UbiComp* (2013), pp. 315–324
2. D. Philipp, P. Baier, C. Dibak, F. Drr, K. Rothermel, S. Becker, M. Peter, D. Fritsch, Mapgenie: Grammar-enhanced indoor map construction from crowd-sourced data, in *PerCom* (2014), pp. 139–147

3. G. Shen, Z. Chen, P. Zhang, T. Moscibroda, Y. Zhang, Walkie-markie: Indoor pathway mapping made easy, in *NSDI* (2013), pp. 85–98
4. H. Shin, Y. Chon, H. Cha, Unsupervised construction of an indoor floor plan using a smartphone. IEEE Trans. Syst. Man Cybern. Part C Appl. Rev. **42**(6), 889–898 (2012)
5. R. Faragher, R. Harle, Smartslam-an efficient smartphone indoor positioning system exploiting machine learning and opportunistic sensing, in *ION GNSS+* (2014)
6. J. Huang, D. Millman, M. Quigley, D. Stavens, S. Thrun, A. Aggarwal, Efficient, generalized indoor wifi graphslam, in *IEEE ICRA* (2011), pp. 1038–1043
7. M. Alzantot, M. Youssef, Crowdinside: automatic construction of indoor floorplans, in *SIGSPA-TIAL* (2012), pp. 99–108
8. R. Gao, M. Zhao, T. Ye, F. Ye, Y. Wang, K. Bian, T. Wang, X. Li, Jigsaw: Indoor floor plan reconstruction via mobile crowdsensing, in *ACM MobiCom* (2014), pp. 249–260
9. J. Manweiler, P. Jain, R.R. Choudhury, Satellites in our pockets: an object positioning system using smartphones, in *MobiSys* (2012), pp. 211–224
10. J. Canny, A computational approach to edge detection. IEEE Trans. Pattern Anal. Mach. Intell. **8**(6), 679–698 (1986)
11. C. Rother, A new approach to vanishing point detection in architectural environments, in *BMVC*, (2000), pp. 382–391
12. D.C. Lee, M. Hebert, T. Kanade, Geometric reasoning for single image structure recovery, in *IEEE CVPR* (2009), pp. 2136–2143
13. A. Rai, K.K. Chintalapudi, V.N. Padmanabhan, R. Sen, Zee: zero-effort crowdsourcing for indoor localization, in *ACM MobiCom* (2012), pp. 293–304
14. H. Wang, S. Sen, A. Elgohary, M. Farid, M. Youssef, R.R. Choudhury, No need to war-drive: Unsupervised indoor localization, in *ACM MobiSys* (2012), pp. 197–210
15. P. Zhou, M. Li, G. Shen, Use it free: instantly knowing your phone attitude, in *ACM MobiCom* (2014), pp. 605–616
16. D. Gusenbauer, C. Isert, J. Krosche, Self-contained indoor positioning on off-the-shelf mobile devices, in *IEEE IPIN* (2010)
17. M. Ester, H.-P. Kriegel, J. Sander, X. Xu, A density-based algorithm for discovering clusters in large spatial databases with noise, in *AAAI KDD* (1996), pp. 226–231
18. G. Einicke, L. White, Robust extended kalman filtering. IEEE Trans. Signal Process. (1999)
19. M. Montemerlo, S. Thrun, D. Koller, B. Wegbreit, Fastslam: a factored solution to the simul-taneous localization and mapping problem, in *AAAI* (2002), pp. 593–598
20. D.G. Lowe, Object recognition from local scale-invariant features, in *IEEE ICCV* (1999), pp. 1150–1157
21. S. Thrun, Learning occupancy grid maps with forward sensor models. Auton. Robots **15**(2), 111–127 (2003)
22. S. Chen, M. Li, K. Ren, X. Fu, C. Qiao, Rise of the indoor crowd: Reconstruction of building interior view via mobile crowdsourcing, in *ACM SenSys* (2015)
23. Amazon mechanical turk. https://www.mturk.com
24. Gigwalk. http://www.gigwalk.com
25. Mobileworks. https://www.mobileworks.com
26. Crowdflower. http://www.crowdflower.com
27. X. Zhang, G. Xue, R. Yu, D. Yang, J. Tang, Truthful incentive mechanisms for crowdsourcing, in *IEEE INFOCOM* (2015), pp. 2830–2838
28. J. Chung, M. Donahoe, C. Schmandt, I. Kim, P. Razavai, M. Wiseman, Indoor location sensing using geo-magnetism, in *MobiSys* (2011), pp. 141–154
29. L. Li, G. Shen, C. Zhao, T. Moscibroda, J.-H. Lin, F. Zhao, Experiencing and handling the diversity in data density and environmental locality in an indoor positioning service, in *ACM MobiCom* (2014), pp. 459–470
30. N. Roy, H. Wang, R.R. Choudhury, I am a smartphone and i can tell my users walking direction, in *ACM MobiSys* (2014), pp. 329–342
31. A. Sankar, S. Seitz, Capturing indoor scenes with smartphones, in *ACM UIST* (2012), pp. 403–412

32. S. Chen, M. Li, K. Ren, C. Qiao, Crowdmap: accurate reconstruction of indoor floor plans from crowdsourced sensor-rich videos, in *IEEE ICDCS* (2015)
33. A.T. Mariakakis, S. Sen, J. Lee, K.-H. Kim, Sail: single access point-based indoor localization, in *ACM MobiSys* (2014), pp. 315–328
34. I. Simon, S.M. Seitz, S. Agarwal, N. Snavely, R. Szeliski, Building rome in a day, in *ICCV* (2009)
35. J. Dong, Y. Xiao, M. Noreikis, Z. Ou, A. Ylä-Jääski, iMoon: Using smartphones for image-based indoor navigation, in *ACM SenSys* (2015)
36. Project tango tablet hardware. https://developers.google.com/project-tango/hardware/tablet# technical_specifications
37. S. Izadi, D. Kim, O. Hilliges, D. Molyneaux, R. Newcombe, P. Kohli, J. Shotton, S. Hodges, D. Freeman, A. Davison et al., Kinectfusion: real-time 3d reconstruction and interaction using a moving depth camera, in *ACM UIST* (2011), pp. 559–568
38. K. Konolige, M. Agrawal, Frameslam: from bundle adjustment to real-time visual mapping. IEEE Trans. Robot. **24**(5), 1066–1077 (2008)
39. B. Ferris, D. Fox, N.D. Lawrence, Wifi-slam using gaussian process latent variable models, in *IJCAI*, vol. 7 (2007), pp. 2480–2485

Chapter 4
Indoor Localization by Photo-Taking of the Environment

Abstract Mainstream indoor localization technologies rely on RF signatures that require extensive human efforts to measure and periodically recalibrate signatures. The progress to ubiquitous localization remains slow. In this chapter, we explore Sextant, an alternative approach that leverages environmental reference objects such as store logos. A user uses a smartphone to obtain relative position measurements to such static reference objects for the system to triangulate the user location. Sextant leverages image matching algorithms to automatically identify the chosen reference objects by photo-taking, and we propose two methods to systematically address image matching mistakes that cause large localization errors. We formulate the benchmark image selection problem, prove its NP-completeness, and propose a heuristic algorithm to solve it. We also propose a couple of geographical constraints to further infer unknown reference objects. To enable fast deployment, we propose a lightweight site survey method for service providers to quickly estimate the coordinates of reference objects. Extensive experiments have shown that Sextant prototype achieves 2–5 m accuracy at 80-percentile, comparable to the industry state of the art, while covering a 150 × 75 m mall and 300 × 200 m train station requires a one-time investment of only 2–3 man-hours from service providers.

4.1 Introduction

Indoor localization [1–3] is the basis for novel features in various location-based applications. Despite more than a decade of research, localization service is not yet pervasive indoors. The latest industry state of the art, Google Indoor Maps [4], covers about 10,000 locations in 18 countries, which are only a fraction of the millions of shopping centers, airports, train stations, museums, hospitals, and retail stores on the planet.

One major obstacle behind the sporadic availability is that current mainstream indoor localization technologies largely rely on RF (Radio Frequency) signatures from certain IT infrastructure (e.g., WiFi access points [1, 2] and cellular towers [5]). Additionally, obtaining the *signature map* usually requires dedicated labor efforts to measure the signal parameters at fine-grained grid points. Because they are

© The Author(s) 2018
R. Gao et al., *Smartphone-Based Indoor Map Construction*,
SpringerBriefs in Computer Science, https://doi.org/10.1007/978-981-10-8378-5_4

susceptible to intrinsic fluctuations and external disturbances, the signatures have to be recalibrated periodically to ensure accuracy. Some recent research [6–8] has started to leverage crowdsourcing to reduce site survey efforts, but incentives are still lacking for wide user adoption. Thus the progress is inevitably slow.

Localization also requires more than mere network connectivity. For example, six strongest towers are usually needed [5] for GSM localization, but the obstruction of walls may deprive many places signals from enough number of towers. WiFi localization also requires enough number of access points in signatures to effectively distinguish different locations. Thus, places with network connectivity may not always be conducive to localization.

In this chapter, we explore an alternative approach that has comparable performance but without relying on the RF signature. Specifically, we leverage environmental *physical features*, such as logos of stores or paintings on the walls, as *reference objects*. Users use the smartphone to measure their relative positions to physical features, and the coordinates of these reference objects are used to compute user locations. This has a few advantages: (1) Physical features are part of and abundant in the environment; they do not require dedicated deployment and maintenance efforts like IT infrastructure; (2) They seldom move and usually remain static over long periods of time. They are not affected by and thus impervious to electromagnetic disturbances from microwaves, cordless phones, or wireless cameras. Once measured, their coordinates do not change, thus eliminating the need for periodic recalibration.

The realization of such benefits, however, turns out to be a nontrivial journey. First, we need to identify a suitable form of relative position that can be effectively measured by smartphones with accuracies favorable for localization. Second, the abundance of physical features is not always a blessing: users need some guidelines to decide which ones to measure for smaller localization errors. Third, to enable fast deployment, service providers have to obtain the coordinates of reference objects in a new environment with low human efforts. Finally, the system has to know which reference objects are selected by users. Relying on explicit user input can be a nonstarter. Ideally, the system should gain such input with as little efforts from users as possible.

Our investigation leads us to the localization method of *Sextant*.[1] In the prototype we build on smartphones [9], the user takes a picture for each of three nearby reference objects one by one. The photos are matched against the benchmark images of each reference object, to identify which reference objects are selected; thus their coordinates, together with relative position measurements, are used to triangulate the user's location.

The main source of inaccuracy in Sextant is the imperfection of image matching algorithms. Their accuracy is affected significantly by which images are used as benchmark for reference objects. An image taken from extreme angles or distances may lead to significant matching errors. Then, the system does not have the

---

[1] Sextant is commonly used by sailors to determine their longitude/latitude by measuring the angle between visible objects, usually celestial ones like the Sun.

coordinates of the correct reference objects for localization. Had the matching been perfect, Sextant could have achieved much higher accuracy.

Thus, we also propose two methods to systematically address the image matching errors [10]. First, we study how to select the best images as the benchmark when multiple candidate images are available for each reference object. The purpose is to minimize "cross matching" where one reference object's photo is incorrectly matched to the benchmark of another. Second, we impose additional constraints to correct wrong matching results. This is based on the observation that those reference objects chosen by the user are usually close to each other. Given even one correct match, the unknown reference objects can be inferred with much higher probability from a nearby range. Prototype experiments in large indoor environments have shown promising results, with 80-percentile accuracy at 2–5 m, comparable to Google Indoor Maps (~7 m).

Our Sextant prototype is described in Fig. 4.1. Service provider selects certain benchmark images for each reference object, and estimates their coordinates; photos and gyro data from user smartphones are used as inputs in Sextant system. Sextant leverages image matching techniques to identify those chosen reference objects, infers the unknown ones after user feedback, and then computes user location using a triangulation method.

We make the following contributions in this work:

- We identify a form of relative position measurement and its respective triangulation method suitable for modern smartphone hardware. We also analyze the localization errors and devise a simple rule of reference object selection to minimize errors.

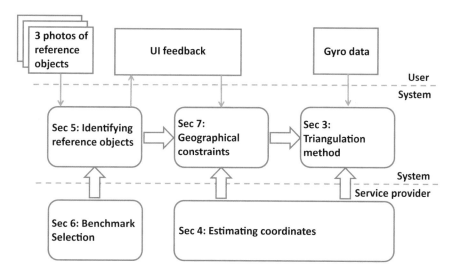

Fig. 4.1 Relationship among different components in Sextant prototype. Each component uses images or gyro data and output from the previous component

- We leverage image matching techniques to identify the chosen reference objects, formulate their benchmark selection as a combinatorial optimization problem, and prove its NP-completeness. We then propose and evaluate a heuristic algorithm based on iterative perturbation for realistic solutions.
- We propose a lightweight site survey method such that a service provider can quickly obtain the coordinates of reference objects in a previously unmapped environment with reasonable accuracy ($\sim$1 m at 80-percentile). Our experiments find that it takes a *one-time* investment of 2–3 man-hours to survey a 150×75 m shopping mall or a 300×200 m train station.
- We propose several geographical constraints that help make much informed decision about the identities of incorrectly matched reference objects. Together they greatly improve the inference accuracy of the system.
- We build a Sextant prototype, and conduct extensive experiments in large complex indoor environments that shows 2–5 m accuracy at 80-percentile using the estimated coordinates, which are comparable to the industry state of the art.

In the rest of the chapter, we study the forms of relative positions and the accuracies of suitable sensors (Sect. 4.2). We then describe the localization operations, study the optimal reference object selection, and demonstrate the feasibility of the operations as a localization primitive (Sect. 4.3). We propose a lightweight approach for estimating the coordinates in an unmapped environment (Sect. 4.4), describe the automatic recognition of chosen reference objects using image matching algorithm (Sect. 4.5), address the benchmark selection problem for reference objects (Sect. 4.6), and use geographical constraints to lower localization errors caused by image matching mistakes (Sect. 4.7). We discuss our limits (Sect. 4.8), review related work (Sect. 4.9), and then conclude the chapter (Sect. 4.10).

4.2   Relative Position Measurement

Relative positions include the distance and orientation between the user and the reference object. Although smartphones can measure their pairwise distance easily [11], they are not equipped with a sensor to directly measure the distance to a physical object. While orientation can take two forms, *absolute and relative angles*, both of which can be used to triangulate the user.

Absolute angle based localization. As shown in Fig. 4.5, given the coordinates of two reference objects R_1, R_2 and the absolute angle α, β (w.r.t. an axis in the coordinate system), the user P is at the intersection of two rays from R_1, R_2.

Relative angle based localization. Given the coordinates of two reference objects R_2, R_3 and the relative angle α (i.e., $\angle R_2 P R_3$) between them, the edge $R_2 R_3$ and α can uniquely determine a circle where $R_2 R_3$ is the subtense and α is the interior angle (see Fig. 4.6). The user is located along the arc of the circle. With three such reference objects (R_1, R_2, R_3) and two relative angles (α, β), two circles are determined and the user P is at the intersection of the circles.

Modern smartphones are usually equipped with a digital compass that gives the absolute angle with respect to geographic north, and a gyroscope that measures the

Fig. 4.2 Compass/gyroscope drifts (in degrees °) when moving the phone along a straight line

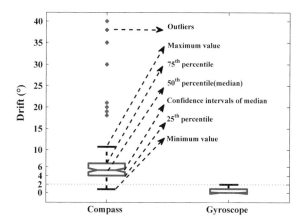

rotated angle of the phone between two positions.[2] Although there has been some reports [8] on the error of the compass, it is not immediately clear to us whether the accuracies of the compass and gyroscope are consistent under various factors. To this end, we conduct an experiment using an iPhone 4 in a 20.4 m × 6.6 m office area where 50 test locations are evenly distributed.

Moving the phone along a straight line. When the phone is moved along a one-meter straight line at 25 cm step lengths (shown in Fig. 4.7a), the compass or gyroscope readings are expected to remain the same. Thus the *drift*, the difference of two consecutive sensor readings, should be close to zero. From Fig. 4.2, we can see that the compass has quite significant drifts (e.g., 6° at 75-percentile); it also has large outliers (e.g., 18–40°) due to electromagnetic disturbances such as nearby electric wires. However, the gyroscope has consistently small (e.g., maximum at 2°) drifts.

Rotating the phone on radial lines. Next we align the phone along radial lines separated by 30° in a semicircle (shown in Fig. 4.7b). We define the *measured angle* (expected to be close to 30°) between two adjacent radial lines as the difference between two respective sensor readings. The *drift* is how much the measured angle deviates from 30°. From Fig. 4.3, we make similar observations to those of Fig. 4.2. The gyroscope still has consistently small drifts while the compass is unsuitable for accurate angle measurements.

Time, building, orientation, and rotation speed. We repeat the second experiment for the gyroscope at 10 AM, 2 PM and 10 PM, and in rooms of three buildings (classroom, lab, indoor stadium). From Fig. 4.4, we find similar small drifts (~1°). We place the phone at a test location, and point the phone to four vertically intersected directions, east, south, west, and north (as shown in Fig. 4.7a). Then, we rotate the phone by $\pm d°$ where $-d°$ is a clockwise and $+d°$ a counterclockwise rotation,

---

[2]To be exact, the gyroscope measures the rotation rates of the phone in radian/sec around its x-, y-, and z-axes. The angle is obtained by integrating the rotation rate against time between the two positions.

Fig. 4.3 Compass/gyroscope drifts (in degree °) when the phone is placed on radial lines

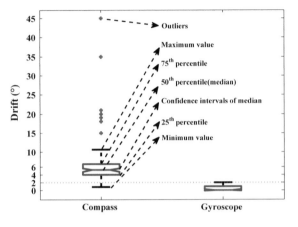

Fig. 4.4 Gyroscope drifts (in degree °) versus time of the day and building types

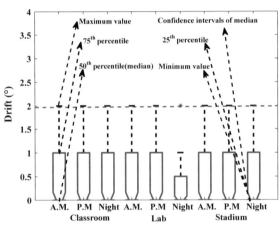

Fig. 4.5 Absolute angle based

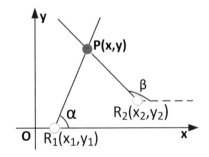

Fig. 4.6 Relative angle based

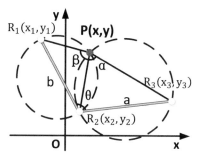

and $d = 15, 30, 45$. This is repeated three times. We find that the error is at most $1°$ and more than half of them have less than $1°$ errors. We place the phone at a fixed location, and rotate the phone at two different speeds, finishing a $10°$ rotation in 2 and 5 seconds. This is intended to see how it behaves under different user operations. Again, we find consistently small drift in both cases (Fig. 4.7).

From the above study, we find that the compass has quite large drifts caused by ferromagnetic materials (e.g., magnets, floor tiles, decorative marble) and electrical objects (e.g., electric appliances, electric wires under the floor), whose disturbances are impossible to eliminate. Thus, we conclude that the gyroscope has consistently high level of accuracy, and decide to use the relative angle based localization as shown in Fig. 4.6.

4.3 Triangulation Method

4.3.1 User Operations and Location Computation

Given the triangulation method in Sextant, the user needs to measure two relative angles between three reference objects (Fig. 4.6). He can stand at his current location, spin his body and arm to point the phone to these reference objects one by one (as illustrated in Fig. 4.8). Given the two angles α, β and the coordinates of the three reference objects (as illustrated in Fig. 4.6), the user location can be computed as follows[3]:

$$\begin{cases} x = x_0 \dfrac{x_3 - x_2}{a} - y_0 \dfrac{y_3 - y_2}{a} + x_2, \\ y = x_0 \dfrac{y_3 - y_2}{a} + y_0 \dfrac{x_3 - x_2}{a} + y_2, \end{cases} \qquad (4.1)$$

---

[3]Because an object (e.g., a door) might be large, pointing to different parts (e.g., left vs. right edge) can incur different angle readings. We impose a *default convention* of always pointing to the horizontal center of an object.

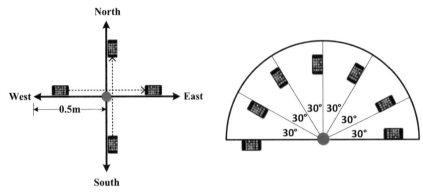

(a) The phone is moved along a straight line, and the dot represents a test location;

(b) The phone is placed on the radial lines of a semi-circle, and the dot at the center represents a test location.

Fig. 4.7 Two experimental scenarios for angle measurements using smartphones

Fig. 4.8 The main steps of user operations: three reference objects are chosen by the user; two rotated angles α and β are measured by the phone gyroscope. Assuming the coordinates of O, A and B are known, the user's location can be calculated

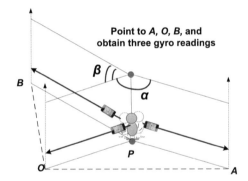

where

$$
\begin{cases}
a = \sqrt{(x_3 - x_2)^2 + (y_3 - y_2)^2}, \\
b = \sqrt{(x_1 - x_2)^2 + (y_1 - y_2)^2}, \\
x_0 = \dfrac{ab[\sin(\beta+\theta)\cot\alpha+\cos(\beta+\theta)][a\sin\beta\cot\alpha+b\cos(\beta+\theta)]}{[b\sin(\beta+\theta)-a\sin\beta]^2+[b\cos(\beta+\theta)+a\sin\beta\cot\alpha]^2}, \\
y_0 = \dfrac{ab[\sin(\beta+\theta)\cot\alpha+\cos(\beta+\theta)][b\sin(\beta+\theta)-a\sin\beta]}{[b\sin(\beta+\theta)-a\sin\beta]^2+[b\cos(\beta+\theta)+a\sin\beta\cot\alpha]^2}, \\
\theta = \arccos\left[\dfrac{(x_3-x_2)(x_1-x_2)+(y_3-y_2)(x_3-x_2)}{ab}\right]
\end{cases}
\tag{4.2}
$$

For the above operations to become a reliable localization primitive, we need to address localization errors from two more sources other than angle measurements (studied in Sect. 4.2): (1) We use obvious environmental features such as store logos as reference points. In a complex environment, most locations have multiple of them around. The user needs to select three that lead to smaller localization errors. (2)

The error introduced by imperfections in user pointing (e.g., various wrist/arm/foot gestures) and device hardware. We study these two issues in the next two subsections.

4.3.2 Criteria for Users to Choose Reference Objects

Impact of rotated angle drift. To understand the impact of the drift on localization errors, we conduct a numerical simulation for an a m $\times$ b m rectangle area with four corners as reference objects. We repeat the localization computation at a grid of test locations at $(m\delta, n\delta)$ where δ is the grid cell size, and $m \in [1, a/\delta]$, $n \in [1, b/\delta]$. Although this is a rather simplified case, we want to find guidelines for combinations of reference objects that lead to higher localization accuracy.

We use Skewness/Kurtosis tests (a.k.a. SK-test) [12] on the gyroscope readings and find that the drift conforms to normal distribution. The mean is close to zero, and the 95% confidence interval is about $\pm 6°$. Thus, we use $\pm 6°$ to evaluate worst-case localization errors in the following simulation.

Choose a fixed set of reference objects. We first study a simple rule: always choose a fixed set of three reference objects (e.g., corner A, O, B). We set the area size $a = 10, b = 5$, grid size $\delta = 0.2$, then vary the drift as $\Delta\alpha = 0, \pm 6°$, $\Delta\beta = 0, \pm 6°$, and show the average localization error of the eight combinations of $\Delta\alpha$ and $\Delta\beta$ (except $\Delta\alpha = \Delta\beta = 0$) in Fig. 4.9a as a 3-d plot. We observe that the localization error is small (e.g., <1 m) when the test location is close to the center reference object O; it becomes much larger when the location moves farther away from object O. We observe similar patterns with areas of other sizes and drifts of other values.

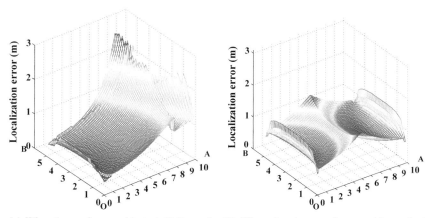

(a) When three reference objects A, O, B are always chosen;

(b) When the closest reference object rule is used.

Fig. 4.9 Average localization error when $\Delta\alpha$, $\Delta\beta = 0, \pm 6°$

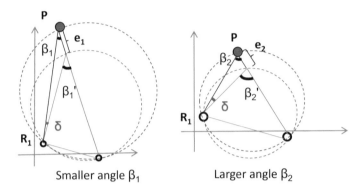

Smaller angle β_1 Larger angle β_2

Fig. 4.10 The same angle drift δ on a smaller angle β_1 causes a larger localization error e_1 than that on a larger angle β_2, because the longer $\overline{R_1 P}$ distance leads to more displacement

Small acute angles lead to larger errors. Intuitively, a distant test location tends to have a small acute angle between two reference objects. The distant location can have a larger displacement while still incurring a small angle drift. As illustrated in Fig. 4.10, the same error δ is added to two angle measurements β_1 and β_2. The localization error is roughly how much the user location P can move when the radial line $R_1 P$ rotates angle δ around center R_1. Over the same rotated angle δ, a larger radius leads to longer displacement of P, thus larger localization error. We have conducted further tests and validated the intuition. This is similar to GDOP in GPS localization [13].

Closest Reference Object Rule. From the above observation, we come up with a simple rule: choose the closest reference object and its left, right adjacent ones as three reference objects. Such closer objects lead to larger angles, thus avoiding the small acute angles that cause large localization errors. We repeat the simulation using this simple rule in the same rectangle area. Figures 4.9b shows that the average localization error is no more than 1 m at all test locations. This clearly demonstrates the effectiveness of this simple rule. Simulations of other area sizes also confirm our discovery.

4.3.3 Robustness of the Localization Primitive

We further investigate the impact of a number of practical factors on localization error. We find that all of them can be addressed and the operations described in Sect. 4.3.1 can be made a robust primitive for localization.

Impact of pointing gestures. To study the error caused by various user pointing gestures, we recruit ten volunteers to point using three types of gestures with an iPhone4. The first two types require a user to stand still and only spin his arm or wrist to point to objects; the third requires a user to spin his body and arm together.

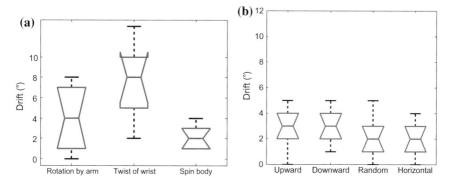

Fig. 4.11 The rotated angle drift under: **a** various types of users' pointing gestures, and **b** different pointing altitude

Figure 4.11a shows the angle drift from each type of gesture. By only twisting the wrist, users make relatively large errors ($\sim 8°$), while spinning body and arm leads to the least error ($\sim 2°$). Thus, we recommend the third gesture for pointing.

Impact of the phone's altitude. While spinning the arm, a user may not be able to keep the phone in a horizontal plane. He may unwittingly raise or lower the phone. Thus, the difference between two gyroscope readings may not accurately reflect the horizontal rotated angle. To avoid such inaccuracies, we use the horizontal component of the gyroscope readings to accurately measure the angle in the horizontal plane.

We recruit four test groups of users to point the phone with different altitude trajectories: (1/2) raise/lower the phone with a random upwards/downwards altitude; (3) randomly raise and lower the phone during rotation; and (4) absolutely horizontal using a water level device. From Fig. 4.11b, we observe that the average angle drift in the two groups of "upwards" and "downwards" is just $1°$ more than those in the other two groups, owing to our method of calculation using the horizontal component. In the following experiments, we also find that the pointing altitude trajectories have little impact on localization errors. We ask the same four test groups of users to repeat the experiments in the meeting room mentioned in Fig. 4.12, the 90-percentile accuracy is below 0.5 m for all groups.

Impact of the area size, shape, and reference object width. We conduct experiments in two rectangle areas (a 6.6 m × 4.2 m meeting room and a 14.4 m × 13.2 m hospital hall). We use the closest reference object rule and repeat the experiment three times at each test location on a grid of $\sim$1 m cell size. The CDFs of average errors are shown in Fig. 4.12. We find that the 80-percentile accuracy is around 0.2 m and 0.6 m, respectively. Due to the linear scaling, the larger hall has slightly larger errors.

We test in a polygon room (roughly 7.6 m × 5.7m) and find similar results (e.g., 0.7 m at 90-percentile). We also test in two large outdoor areas of 30 m × 30 m and 20 m × 40 m sizes. The 80-percentile error is $\sim$1 m and maximum at 1.5 m, slightly larger than that of indoor environments because it scales to the area size. Finally, we

Fig. 4.12 The CDF of error
distribution for two rectangle
rooms

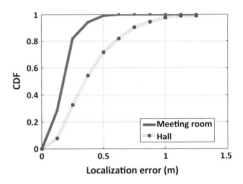

try reference objects of some widths (e.g., 1 m wide posters), and find that when users aim at the center of reference objects during pointing, the accuracy is not affected much (~0.5 m for 90-percentile). The above shows that the pointing primitive's accuracies are not affected much by the size, shape of the enclosing area, and widths of reference objects.

Impact of user efforts. How carefully the user points to reference objects inevitably influences the accuracy of angle measurements. We employ three groups of users to evaluate the impact of user efforts: "normal" users use the closest reference object rule and point with certain care; "savvy" users pay more attention to measure the angles very carefully; while "impatient" users tend to finish the operations quickly and cursorily.

Figure 4.13 shows the CDF results in the meeting room. We make several observations: a savvy user obtains the best accuracy (e.g., ~0.3 m for 90-percentile); a normal user can achieve comparable accuracy; and an impatient user has lower but still reasonable accuracy with the closest reference object rule (e.g., 0.9 m at 90-percentile). These show that: (1) The pointing primitive can achieve reasonable accuracy with various degrees of use efforts; and (2) the closest reference object is an

Fig. 4.13 The CDF of error
distribution by different
types of users

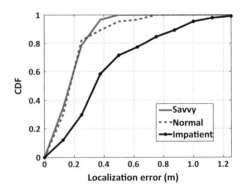

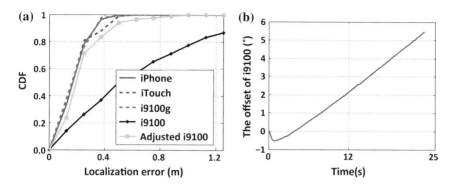

Fig. 4.14 Experiments using different types of devices in the meeting room. **a** The CDF of error distribution, and **b** Angle drift versus time for i9100

effective rule of thumb. We repeat the same experiments in the hall and have similar observations with that in the meeting room.

Impact of mobile device hardware. Gyroscope in different phones has varying qualities. We pick four popular devices (iPhone4, iTouch4, Samsung i9100, Samsung i9100g) to compare their performance. Figure 4.14a shows that iPhone4, iTouch4, and i9100g almost have the same expected performance at a high level of accuracy (e.g., ∼0.4 m at 90-percentile). However, i9100 shows the worst results (over 1.2 m).

We place the i9100 phone at a static location and record the readings once the gyroscope is turned on (at time 0 in Fig. 4.14b). We find the value declines at the very beginning, and then starts increasing (as shown in Fig. 4.14b). This is caused by the relatively lower quality of the STMicroelectroinics K3G gyroscope in i9100. To compensate for such intrinsic drifts, we use curve fitting methods to derive equations that characterize the variations over time to calibrate the gyroscope reading. We then repeat the experiments and the results ("Adjusted i9100" curve in Fig. 4.14a) show that after calibration, it has accuracy comparable to the other three devices. For the other devices i9100g, iPhone4, iTouch4, same experiments are repeated and the curves tend to be flat horizontal lines, showing little drift over time.

From the above study, we conclude that the pointing operations can be made a robust localization primitive provided that the user follows the guidelines with certain care. In the next two sections, we investigate how a service provider can quickly obtain the coordinates of reference objects, and how the system can gain input of which reference objects the user has chosen.

4.4 Site Survey for Reference Objects Coordinates

Sextant needs the coordinates of reference objects to compute user location. The most straightforward method is to manually measure the distances, thus coordinates directly. Although this is a one-time investment because reference objects do not move, it still consumes time when there are many of them. In this section, we present a method for a service provider to significantly reduce the human effort.

4.4.1 Location Estimation in Unmapped Environments

In an unmapped environment, two workers[4] of a service provider first choose two *pairwise visible* reference objects, say A and B respectively, called *starting pairs* (step1 in Fig. 4.15). The two workers stand at A and B respectively, then measure the distance a between them (e.g., by counting floor tiles, using a tape measure or techniques such as BeepBeep [11]). We can set a coordinate system with A at the origin $(0, 0)$ and B at $(a, 0)$. We call objects A and B as *positioned* objects.

Then, the workers select a third *unpositioned* object C and determine its coordinates (x, y). When C is visible from A and B, the worker at A points the phone to B, and then C to measure $\angle BAC$. Similarly, the other worker can measure $\angle ABC$. The two angles $\alpha = \angle BAC$ and $\beta = \angle ABC$ can be used to calculate the coordinates of C: $x = (a \tan \beta)/(\tan \alpha + \tan \beta)$, and $y = (a \tan \alpha \tan \beta)/(\tan \alpha + \tan \beta)$.

The positioned object C together with A and B form a triangle, and the distance $\overline{AC}$ (or $\overline{BC}$) can be easily derived using the estimated coordinates of C. The worker at A can then move to C, and repeat similar processes to locate additional objects D, E (steps 2 and 3 in Fig. 4.15), and so on. The coordinates of each additional positioned object can be uniquely determined in this coordinate system.

Blocked positioned objects. During the process when the direct line of sight between B and C is blocked (step2-b in Fig. 4.15), one of $\overline{BD}$, $\overline{CD}$ plus angle $\angle BDC$ are measured, together with $\overline{BC}$ (known already), the coordinates of D can be determined by the law of sines.

Fig. 4.15 Procedure to estimate the coordinates of reference objects

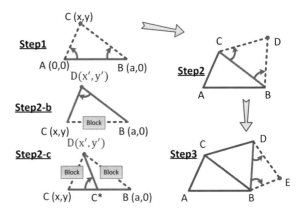

_____

[4]The procedure can be conducted by one worker with more walking, or multiple workers in parallel.

Blocked unpositioned objects. When an unpositioned object D is blocked from both B and C (step2-c in Fig. 4.15), one worker has to move along the line between C and B to find an appropriate location C^* where object D is visible. They measure distance $\overline{CC^*}$, the angle $\gamma = \angle CC^*D$, and $\overline{C^*D}$ to locate D relative to C, thus eventually its coordinates. We omit the case when D is blocked from only one of B, C, which is similar to step2-b.

New starting pairs to control the error accumulation. One problem arises from such hop-by-hop estimation: the coordinates of a new object may contain error; when they are used to position another object, the error may grow. To control such accumulation, a simple method is to use a new starting pair after a few hops to reset the error back to zero.

4.4.2   Experiments on Site Survey

We conduct experiments in two large indoor environments, a 150×75 m shopping mall (Fig. 4.16a) and a 300×200 m train station (Fig. 4.16b).

Accuracy. When only one starting pair is used (reference points {①⑥} in Fig. 4.16a and {①⑬} in Fig. 4.16b, shown in green or slightly darker color), errors are small (<2 m) up to $4 \sim 6$ hops away, beyond which they quickly grow to more than 12 m. Obviously such large errors are not acceptable. After we add 2, 3 more starting pairs in these two environments ({⑦⑨} and {⑲⑳} in the mall, {㉗㊷}, {⑰⑲} and {⑧⑨} in the station), the 80-percentile errors are within $1m$, while the maximum about 2 m (Fig. 4.16c). They eventually lead to satisfactory localization accuracy.

Human efforts. In the mall, each of the 63 reference objects takes about 2 min to measure the angle(s) and/or distance(s); in the station each of the 53 objects takes about 3 minutes due to longer walking distances. In total they cost 2, 2.6 man-hours. Assuming WiFi signatures are measured 2 m apart and each location takes 10s, excluding inaccessible areas 5,200 m^2 and 23,700 m^2 areas need to be covered, resulting in 3.6, 16.5 man-hours. Thus the cost is roughly 16–55% that of WiFi. Note that over long time WiFi incurs periodic recalibration costs each of similar amounts, while we pay only a one-time effort.

If brute-force measurements are used, each reference point takes 50% more time when regular floor tiles are available to count the coordinates; otherwise using a tape measure can triple the time. Although the quantifications are quite rough, they show that our site survey method can significantly reduce the human efforts compared to those of brute-force or WiFi.

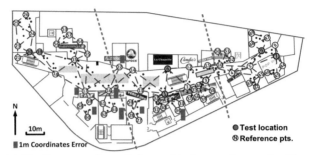

(a) The floor map of a mall dissected in three sections each with a starting pair, in total 63 reference objects and 108 test locations.

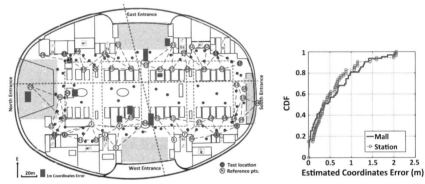

(b) The floor map of a train station dissected in four sections each with a starting pair, in total 53 reference objects and 46 test locations.

(c) Errors in estimated coordinates for a mall and train station.

Fig. 4.16 Floor map of a mall (**a**) and station (**b**), as well as their estimated coordinates errors (**c**). The vertical bars on (**a**) and (**b**) show the errors in estimated coordinates; those <1 m are not shown

4.5 Identifying Chosen Reference Objects

The Sextant system has to know which reference objects are selected by the user. However, it is impractical to require every user to explicitly tell the system about her/his choice. Thus, how to identify chosen reference objects with less user efforts becomes a quite challenging problem in a complex environment with many reference objects.

We explore image matching algorithms to handle this issue. The user takes one photo (i.e., test image) for each of the three chosen reference objects one by one, which are matched with benchmark images to identify the corresponding reference objects. Nevertheless, we find that the matching algorithms make wrong identifications in certain situations. Next, we will explain how we use the algorithms and classify error situations in this section. We also address matching errors with some heuristic algorithms in Sects. 4.6 and 4.7.

4.5.1 System Architecture and Workflow

We have prototyped our Sextant system consisting of a smartphone for gyroscope data and image acquisition, a backend server for image matching against a collection of benchmark images of reference objects (taken by a service provider during site survey).

Image capture via finger taps. To accommodate test images taken from different angles, we take three benchmark images for each reference object. The user uses the same spin operations. He taps the phone's screen to take a test image when a chosen reference object is centered on the camera. The tapping also triggers the capture of gyroscope readings. The test image is immediately sent to the server as the user continues for the next reference object.

Image matching and ranking. We examine two most popular image feature vector extraction algorithms, scale-invariant feature transform (SIFT) [14] and speeded up robust features (SURF) [15]. Comparison [15] has shown that SURF is much faster while achieving comparable accuracy to SIFT. Thus, we decide to use SURF in the prototype. Meanwhile, we use the same procedure used in [15] to rank benchmark images based on the number of matched feature vectors. We apply RANdom SAmple Consensus (RANSAC) [16] that uses the relative position constraints among feature vectors to detect and filter wrong feature vector matches.

For each test image, the server ranks the reference objects in descending order of the matching metric, the number of matched feature vectors, and then returns this ranked list of [ID: matching metric value] tuples to the phone. The phone presents the results as a 4×3 thumbnail matrix (Fig. 4.17), with the top row showing the three test images, below each is a column of three best matched reference objects. By default the top match is highlighted. The user can tap the correct one if the top match is wrong. Then the user taps the "confirm" button, and the phone computes the user location based on the corrected matching results and the angles. If none of the top 3 match is correct, the user taps the test image before proceeding with "confirm". The phone applies a heuristic that takes the feedbacks and the ranked list to search for a better match, and displays the final localization result.

Online and Offline Modes. Image matching algorithms inevitably make mistakes. Multiple benchmark images taken from different angles of a reference object improve accuracy significantly. However, more benchmarks lead to higher computing overhead. Thus in Sextant, the number of benchmark images for each reference object is limited to a small number. When many candidate images are available, which images to select as benchmarks to match incoming test images greatly impact the matching accuracy. Thus, we should select the subset of images leading to the best matching accuracy.

In Sextant depending on whether there is network connectivity, the phone can work in online or offline modes. Due to the complexity in image matching algorithms, the preferred location for matching computation is on a backend server. This is when the phone has network connectivity and can upload test images to the server to identify chosen reference objects. This is the online mode.

Fig. 4.17 The UI presented to the user for correction of image matching results. The top row are the three test images taken by the user, below each are the top 3 matched reference objects. The user can denote the correct match by tapping the thumbnail images

It is not uncommon that many locations do not have network connectivity due to the lack of WiFi APs or strong enough cellular signals. Sextant can still work if the computation is done locally. A couple of challenges have to be addressed: (1) The phone must have enough storage to store the benchmark images of reference objects. In reality, we found this is not a problem, and they can be downloaded on demand before the user enters the environment while there is still network connectivity. (2) To reduce the latency, each reference object has to use less, ideally only one benchmark image. Nevertheless we have to provide enough matching accuracy. Thus, the benchmark must be selected carefully to maximize correctness. This is what we address in the offline mode in Sextant.

Data stored on the phone. The implementation requires the phone to store the IDs, coordinates, small image icons, and benchmark images of reference objects. Since each icon is about 3KB, it takes about 200 and 150 KB for 63, 53 reference objects in the mall and train station. An 800×600 benchmark image is only about 30KB, while 50–60 reference objects are sufficient for a large mall or train station. Thus, the total storage is less than 2MB. Such data can be downloaded on demand before the user enters the building. Having the phone doing the localization computation avoids a second interaction to send the corrected results to the server for final results, thus reducing the latency.

4.6 Benchmark Selection of Reference Objects

In Sextant, the user takes one photo (i.e., test image) for each of the three chosen reference objects, which are then matched against benchmark images to identify the corresponding reference objects. We find that the selected benchmarks are crucial in improving image matching accuracy. In this section, we model the benchmark selection problem, prove its NP-completeness, and propose heuristic algorithms to solve it.

4.6.1 Benchmark Selection Problem

We formally define the problem of benchmark selection (notations in Table 4.1): Given m reference objects $\{1, ..., m\}$, and a set of n_i candidate images for reference object i, find one image for each reference object such that the total number of matching errors is minimized.

We denote the decision variables, the labels of the chosen benchmark for each reference object as

$$B = \{b_i | 1 \leq i \leq m, 1 \leq b_i \leq n_i\} \tag{4.3}$$

Given the candidate images, we could profile the number of incorrectly matched images for each reference object, as Fig. 4.18 shows. When reference objects i and j choose x and y as its benchmark respectively, an incorrect match from i to j means an image l for reference object i is incorrectly matched to reference object j. We use $p_{i,x,j,y}$ to denote the number of images for reference object i incorrectly matched to reference object j, and $P = (p_{i,x,j,y})$ as the model given input.

The objective is to find the label selection B that minimizes the number of total incorrectly matched images. We denote C_{obj} as the objective value. Given $P = (p_{i,x,j,y})$, the C_{obj} could be computed by each $B = (b_i)$, as follows:

Table 4.1 RMSE of floor plans (m)

$M = \{1, ..., m\}, i \in M, j \in M$	Reference objects
$N_i = \{1, ..., n_i\}$	Candidate images of reference object i
$B = \{b_i\}$	Label of selected benchmark images for reference object i
$P = \{p_{i,x,j,y}\},$	Number of images for i incorrectly matched
$x \in N_i, y \in N_j$	to j, when x and y are selected benchmark images for i and j respectively.
$K = \{k_{i,x,j,y}\}$	Number of matched feature vectors between image x for i and image y for j
$u(.)$	Unit step function, equals 0 when input is less than 0, and equals 1 otherwise

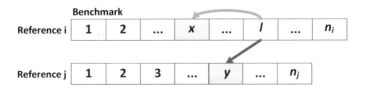

Fig. 4.18 An example of where x and y denote the chosen benchmark (marked yellow) of reference object i and j respectively, and l denotes an image of i being matched to both x and y

$$C_{obj}(B) = \sum_{i \neq j} p_{i,b_i,j,b_j} \qquad (4.4)$$

And $i, j \in \{1, 2, ..., m\}$. Thus our objective is formulated as follows:

$$\min_B C_{obj}(B) \qquad (4.5)$$

4.6.2 NP-Completeness Proof

We formulate its corresponding decision problem, called benchmark selection decision (BSD) problem: Given $P = (p_{i,x,j,y})$ and integer c, determine whether there exists $B = (b_i)$, such that

$$\sum_{i \neq j} p_{i,b_i,j,b_j} \leq c \qquad (4.6)$$

And we denote its instance as $BSD(P, B, c)$.

First, we show that BSD problem belongs to NP. Given its instance, it is easy to verify whether $C_{obj} = \sum_{i \neq j} p_{i,b_i,j,b_j} \leq c$ is satisfied in polynomial time.

To prove BSD problem is NP-complete, we prove that the quadratic assignment problem (QAP), which is known to be NP-complete [17], is reducible in polynomial time to BSD problem. The decision problem of QAP describes that there are two sets: $M = \{0, 1, ..., m - 1\}$ and $N = \{0, 1, ..., m - 1\}$, two functions: $w(i, j) : M \times M \rightarrow R^+$, and $d(x, y) : N \times N \rightarrow R^+$, and a constant c; it determines whether there exists an one-to-one mapping $f : M \rightarrow N$, such that $\sum_{i \neq j} w(i, j) \cdot d(f(i), f(j)) \leq c$.

Based on the following BSD construction, we could reduce the decision problem of QAP to our BSD problem.

$$M = \{0, 1, ..., m - 1\}, \ N = \{0, 1, ..., m - 1\} \tag{4.7}$$

$$i, j \in M, \ x, y \in N \tag{4.8}$$

$$p_{i,x,j,y} = \begin{cases} w(i, j) \cdot d(x, y), if \ x \neq y \\ \eta, if \ x = y \end{cases} \tag{4.9}$$

We set η as a sufficiently large constant, e.g., $\eta = \sum_{i \neq j} \sum_{x,y} w(i, j) \cdot d(x, y)$, to guarantee the solution of BSD problem is a one-to-one mapping from M to N. Its solution also corresponds to the solution of decision problem of QAP.

Thus the BSD problem is NP-complete, and we will present our heuristic algorithm to find an approximated solution in reasonable time.

4.6.3 A Heuristic Algorithm

We here propose a heuristic algorithm to select the best benchmark image for each reference object, the intuition is that the selected image should be similar to other images of its own reference object, and distinct to images of other reference objects.

Profiling. This part is the preparation for our algorithm, aiming to measure the distinction between two candidate images.

According to [15], we first extract feature vectors on each candidate image, and calculate distance between two feature vectors to measure their similarity. The number of matched feature vectors between image x for reference object i and image y for reference object j can be computed beforehand and denoted as

$$K = \{k_{i,x,j,y} | 1 \leq i, j \leq m, 1 \leq x \leq n_i, 1 \leq y \leq n_j\} \tag{4.10}$$

As Fig. 4.18 shows, an image l for i is incorrectly matched to j when it has more matched feature vector with j's benchmark y than with i's benchmark x. Thus $p_{i,x,j,y}$, how many i's images are incorrectly matched to j can be computed as follows:

$$p_{i,x,j,y} = \begin{cases} \sum_{l=1}^{n_i} u(k_{i,l,j,y} - k_{i,l,i,x}), if \ i \neq j \\ 0, if \ i = j \end{cases} \tag{4.11}$$

Thus we could compute P beforehand. Next, we will present how to choose the best benchmark set B, aiming at the minimum objective value C_{obj} which is calculated from Eq. 4.4.

Benchmark initialization. Initially, each reference object is assigned the "best matching" image as its benchmark, meaning its other images are very similar to the benchmark, and the benchmark is very distinct to images of other reference objects.

Thus, its own images match well while other reference objects' images do not match this chosen benchmark. We use two metrics below to measure its similarity to its own reference object's images and its interference to images of other reference objects.

For a chosen benchmark x of reference object i, we use the number of images for i correctly matched to x, rather than chosen benchmark t of reference object j, as the similarity metric. The metric is summed over all possible combinations of $\{j, t\}$ pairs, shown in Eq. 4.12.

$$S_{i,x}^{+} = \frac{1}{n_i} \sum_{s=1}^{n_i} \sum_{j=1}^{m \& j \neq i} \sum_{t=1}^{n_j} u(k_{i,s,i,x} - k_{i,s,j,t}) \tag{4.12}$$

Similarly, we use the number of images for another reference object j incorrectly matched to x, rather than the chosen benchmark t of j, to measure the interference of x to j. This is also summed over all possible combinations of $\{j, t\}$ pairs, shown in Eq. 4.13.

$$S_{i,x}^{-} = \frac{1}{\sum_{j=1}^{m \& j \neq i} n_j} \sum_{j=1}^{m \& j \neq i} \sum_{t=1}^{n_j} \sum_{s=1}^{n_j} u(k_{j,s,i,x} - k_{j,s,j,t}) \tag{4.13}$$

Then, we could score the efficiency of each benchmark x for reference object i, calculated as

$$Score_{i,x} = S_{i,x}^{+} / S_{i,x}^{-} \tag{4.14}$$

For benchmark initialization, we select the image with highest score as the chosen benchmark for reference object i.

Random perturbation. Since the initialization does not necessarily give the overall optimal solution, we use random perturbation to continue improve the solution. Each time we randomly replace a chosen benchmark with an unchosen image of the same reference object, and check if the objective value decreases. If so, we update both the chosen benchmark set and objective value. This is repeated until the objective value decreases less than a threshold C_{th} after X times of continuous replacements. Then, we stop the random perturbation and output the chosen benchmark set. In our implementation, we use $C_{th} = 0$ and $X = 100$.

4.7 Improve Localization with Geographical Constraints

Even with optimized benchmarks, there are still test images whose correct match does not show up in the top 3 results. For such images, we make informed guesses based on an observation: the three chosen reference objects by a user are usually close to each other. We propose two heuristics to estimate unknown reference objects when there are 1 and 2 "uncorrectable" test images.

Algorithm 1 Benchmark selection heuristic algorithm

1: compute $k_{i,x,j,y}$ for each two candidate images;
2: **for** each reference object i **do**
3:     **for** each benchmark x **do**
4:        compute $S_{i,x}^+$ according to Equation (4.12);
5:        compute $S_{i,x}^-$ according to Equation (4.13);
6:        compute $Score_{i,x}$ according to Equation (4.14);
7:     **end for**
8:     $b_i = arg \max Score_{i,x}$;
9: **end for**
10: $time = 0$;
11: **while** $time \leq X$ **do**
12:     randomly select several chosen benchmarks in B, replace each with a random image of its same reference object;
13:     compute objective value C_{obj} according to Equation (4.4);
14:     **if** C_{obj} is decreased **then**
15:        update B based on the random benchmarks;
16:        update C_{obj};
17:        $time = 0$;
18:     **else**
19:        $time + +$;
20:     **end if**
21: **end while**
22: **if** more benchmark is used **then**
23:     **for** each reference object i, j and benchmark x, y **do**
24:        $k_{i,x,j,y} = \max\{k_{i,x,j,y}, \ k_{i,x,j,b_j}\}$;
25:     **end for**
26:     remove B from candidate image set;
27:     go to Step 2 to find the second best benchmark;
28: **end if**

4.7.1 Experiment Results and Problems in Early Prototype

We conduct experiments in two large indoor environments, a 150×75 m shopping mall and a 300×200 m train station. We test our system in both online and offline modes.

Figure 4.19 shows the CDF of localization errors in offline and online modes for both the mall and station. We make a couple observations. First, the online mode has much smaller errors, with 80-percentile localization error within 2 m in mall and 5 m in station. This is because 3 benchmarks are used for each reference object, leading to very high image matching accuracy (e.g., more than 97%). However, the offline mode has 80-percentile error of 14 m in both the mall and station, with large errors reaching tens of meters. This is simply because a single benchmark has much lower matching accuracy even after user feedback. Had all test images been perfectly matched, there would be less than 2 m localization error at 80-percentile in mall and 4 m in station; while the maximum error would be around 5 m both in mall and station. Thus there is quite some space for improvements.

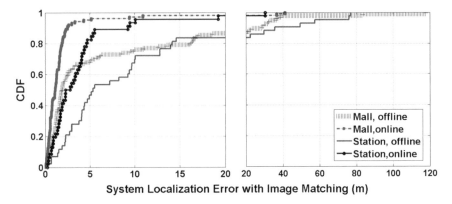

Fig. 4.19 System localization error after the benchmark selection heuristic

4.7.2 Geographical Constraints

To better infer the identity of unknown reference objects whose correct match does not appear in top 3 results, we propose a couple geographical constraints, including cluster partition, distance metric measurement and scoring.

Cluster Partition

Due to the obstructions of walls, some reference objects are unlikely visible to and chosen by the user at the same time. For example, a user in a store can only see reference objects inside but not those outside. If the system knows any correctly matched image inside, the unknown ones must be inside as well.

Accordingly, we cluster reference objects based on geographical layout, e.g., wall obstruction. Thus all objects inside the same store are in one cluster, those outside are in another cluster. Given any correctly matched image, we search the unknown ones within the same cluster using the following two measurements.

Distance Metric Measurement

When two test images are matched to their correct reference objects (denoted as A and B), we find the unknown reference object by computing a metric for each possible reference object X in the same cluster with A and B.

$$D_X = (|AX| + |BX|)/2 \qquad (4.15)$$

When only one image is matched correctly to its reference object A, we compute the following metric for each possible reference object pair X and Y in the same cluster as A.

$$D_{X,Y} = (|AX| + |AY| + |XY|)/3 \qquad (4.16)$$

Scoring

Then, we score the possible candidate(s) according to both their image matching degree and distance metric. The score is defined as follows:

$$score_X = \frac{K_{X,1}}{D_X^2}, \text{ for 1 unknown reference object} \qquad (4.17)$$

$$score_{X,Y} = \frac{K_{X,1} + K_{Y,2}}{D_{X,Y}^2}, \text{ for 2 unknown reference objects} \qquad (4.18)$$

where $K_{i,j}$ is the number of matched feature vectors between the benchmark image(s) of reference object i and the test image of label j ($j = 1$ or 2). The candidate(s) with the highest score is chosen as the unknown reference object(s). The detailed description of the algorithm is shown in Algorithm 2. Note that when there are two unknown reference objects, $score_{X,Y}$ and $score_{Y,X}$ are different due to different pairings between X, Y and test image 1, 2.

Algorithm 2 Heuristic algorithm for geographical constraints

1: cluster reference objects based on geographical layout;
2: find the cluster T of correctly matched reference object(s) after user feedback;
3: **if** number of unknown reference objects=1 **then**
4:    **for** each reference object X in T **do**
5:       compute D_X according to Equation (4.15);
6:       compute $score_X$ according to Equation (4.17);
7:    **end for**
8:    $X_{Est} = arg \max score_X$;
9: **else if** number of unknown reference objects=2 **then**
10:    **for** each reference object pair X,Y in T **do**
11:       compute $D_{X,Y}$ according to Equation (4.16);
12:       compute $score_{X,Y}$ according to Equation (4.18);
13:    **end for**
14:    $\{X_{Est}, Y_{Est}\} = arg \max score_{X,Y}$;
15: **end if**

4.7.3 System Localization Performance

We find that the geographical constraints improve our image matching accuracy to 91.7% (from 82.1%) in the mall and 87.6% (from 81.2%) in the station in offline mode, while 99.4% (from 98.2%) in the mall and 97.9% (from 97.3%) in the station for online use.

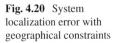

Fig. 4.20 System
localization error with
geographical constraints

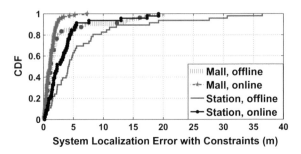

Figure 4.20 shows the CDF of localization errors after the constraints. Compared with earlier system without geographical constraints, localization error is reduced to around 3 m in mall and 8 m in station (both from 14 m) at 80% percentile in offline mode; the maximum error is cut to 20 m (from 118 m) in the mall and 36 m (from 76 m) in the station for offline use. For online use, the 80% error does not reduce much (around 2 m in the mall and 5 m in the station), but the maximum error is lowered to about 7 m (from 41 m) in the mall and 19 m (from 30 m) in the station. These show that the geographical constraints are effective in greatly cutting down maximum error, and improves the general case for offline mode significantly.

4.8 Discussion

Physical features selection for reference objects. Users need to understand which physical features are likely reference objects included by the system. We choose obvious ones such as store logos, information desks and find 50–60 reference objects can cover the mall and train station. However, users may still occasionally pick an object not in the reference object set. Even after the heuristic the system cannot obtain the correct coordinates. We plan to investigate methods to add such objects into the set incrementally.

With the latest techniques on image stitching, users could also take a video during rotating at one place, instead of taking three photos of certain reference objects. In this, we, users, do not need to know what reference objects are and they look like, they only rotate and system will generate a panorama from continuous photos or a video, then system will use the panorama to find if there are reference objects on it, and use our method to localize user.

Disturbances from the surroundings. Occasionally, the illumination inside an indoor building may change during the day, and a test image may have many customers or passengers getting between the user and reference objects. Feature vectors extracted from the test image may be influenced by such dynamic surroundings. Even though the store logos are not blocked, they can disturb the matching algorithm and lead to false match.

Continuous localization. Sextant provides localization after a user completes the operations. It does not yet provide continuous localization when the user is in continuous motion. We plan to investigate how to combine other techniques (e.g., dead reckoning [18]) to infer user locations in moving.

Localizing using more than three reference objects. In principle, more reference objects add more constraints and improve the localization accuracy. It also increases the chances of user localization when one picked object is not in the benchmark set. The costs are more user efforts taking photos and overhead matching images. We will investigate the tradeoff to determine if potential gains outweigh costs.

4.9 Related Work

Smartphone localization has attracted lots attention due to the explosive growth of location-based phone applications. We describe those most relevant to Sextant and provide a comparison that is far from exhaustive.

Signature-based localization. A vast majority of existing research efforts depend on RF signatures from certain IT infrastructure. Following earlier studies that utilize WiFi signals [1, 2] for indoor localization, Liu et al. [3] leverages accurate acoustic ranging estimates among peer phones to aid the WiFi localization for meter level accuracy. Accurate GSM indoor localization is feasible in large multi-floor buildings by using wide signal strength fingerprints that include signal readings from more than 6-strongest cells [5]. Sextant does not rely on such signatures for localization. It uses network connectivity only for computation offloading.

Some work takes advantage of other smartphone sensing modalities for different signatures. SurroundSense [19] combines optical, acoustic, and motion sensors to fingerprint and identifies the logical environment (e.g., stores). UnLoc [20] proposes an unsupervised indoor localization scheme that leverages WiFi, acceleromter, compass, gyroscope, and GPS to identify signature landmarks. Sextant does not use such signatures but static environmental reference objects for triangulating user locations.

Building the signature map. Some recent work has focused on methods for reducing the laborious efforts for building and maintaining signature maps. LiFS [6] leverages the user motion to construct the signature map and crowdsources its calibration to users. EZ [7] proposes genetic-based algorithms to derive the constraints in wireless propagation for configuration-free indoor localization. Zee [8] tracks inertial sensors in mobile devices carried by users while simultaneously performing WiFi scans.

However, since most of those signals are susceptible to intrinsic fluctuations and external disturbances, they must recalibrate the signature map periodically to ensure accuracy. This incurs periodic labor efforts to measure the signal parameters at fine-grained grid points. Compared to these signatures, the physical features (e.g., store logos) we use are static. Sextant only requires a one-time effort to estimate the

coordinates of reference objects, reducing the measurement effort to a fraction of
that of a single WiFi site survey.

Computer vision based work. OPS [21] allows users to locate remote objects
such as buildings by taking a few photos from different known locations. It uses
computer vision algorithms to extract the 3D model of the object and maps it to
ground locations. We use image matching algorithms for identifying chosen reference
objects, not 3D models. We also propose a lightweight site survey method to quickly
estimate the coordinates of reference objects.

SLAM (simultaneous localization and mapping) [22] is a technique for robots to
build the model of a new map and localize themselves within that map simultaneously.
For localization, the robots' kinematics information is needed. Although smartphones
carried by people can provide sensory data, accurate kinematics information remains
a challenge. In computer vision, extracting 3D models could estimate locations based
on captured images. OPS [21] allows users to locate remote objects such as buildings
by taking a few photos from different known locations. Compared to them, our
localization is based on triangulation from angle measurements by the gyroscope.
We use image matching algorithms only for identifying which reference objects are
chosen by the user.

User efforts. Explicit user effort such as body rotation has been adopted for
different purposes recently. Zhang et al. [23] show that the rotation of a user's body
causes dips in received signal strength of a phone, thus providing directions to the
location of an access point. SpinLoc [24] leverages similar phenomena to provide
user localization at accuracies of several meters.

4.10 Conclusion

In this chapter, we explore a new approach that leverages environmental reference
objects to triangulate user locations using relative position measurements from smartphones. Because the reference objects seldom move, it avoids extensive human efforts
in obtaining and maintaining RF signatures in mainstream indoor localization technologies. We have described the triangulation principle, guidelines for reference
object selection and have shown the feasibility of pointing operations as a localization primitive. Then, we propose a lightweight site survey method to quickly estimate
the coordinates of reference objects in unmapped environments. We also adopt image
matching algorithms to automatically identify the selected reference objects by users.

Finally we study two issues: image matching mistakes and inferring unknown
reference objects. We formulate the benchmark selection problem, prove its NP-
completeness, and devise a heuristic algorithm that selects benchmark images of
reference objects for high image matching accuracy. We also propose a couple of
geographical constraints to infer the identities of unknown reference objects that
cannot be corrected by user feedback. Extensive experiments conducted in two large
indoor environments, a 150×75 m shopping mall and a 300×200 m train station,

have demonstrated that Sextant achieves *comparable* performance to the industry state of the art, while requiring only a one-time investment of 2–3 man-hours to survey complex indoor environments hundreds of meters in size.

References

1. P. Bahl, V.N. Padmanabhan, RADAR: an in-building RF-based user location and tracking system, in *IEEE INFOCOM* (2000)
2. M. Youssef, A. Agrawala, The horus wlan location determination system, in *ACM MobiSys* (2005)
3. H. Liu, Y. Gan, J. Yang, S. Sidhom, Y. Wang, Y. Chen, F. Ye, Push the limit of wifi based localization for smartphones, in *ACM Mobicom* (2012)
4. Google Indoor Maps Availability, https://support.google.com/gmm/answer/1685827?hl=en
5. V. Otsason, A. Varshavsky, A. LaMarca, E. de Lara, Accurate gsm indoor localization, in *UbiComp* (2005), pp. 141–158
6. Z. Yang, C. Wu, Y. Liu, Locating in fingerprint space: wireless indoor localization with little human intervention, in *ACM MobiCom* (2012), pp. 269–280
7. K. Chintalapudi, A. Padmanabha Iyer, V.N. Padmanabhan, Indoor localization without the pain, in *ACM MobiCom* (2010)
8. A. Rai, K.K. Chintalapudi, V.N. Padmanabhan, R. Sen, Zee: zero-effort crowdsourcing for indoor localization, in *ACM MobiCom* (2012), pp. 293–304
9. Y. Tian, R. Gao, K. Bian, F. Ye, T. Wang, Y. Wang, X. Li, Towards ubiquitous indoor localization service leveraging environmental physical features, in *IEEE INFOCOM* (2014), pp. 55–63
10. R. Gao, F. Ye, T. Wang, Smartphone indoor localization by photo-taking of the environment, in *IEEE ICC* (2014)
11. C. Peng, G. Shen, Y. Zhang, Y. Li, K. Tan, Beepbeep: a high accuracy acoustic ranging system using cots mobile devices, in *ACM SenSys* (2007)
12. N.L. Johnson, S. Kotz, N. Balakrishnan, *Continuous Univariate Distributions.*, 2nd edn. (Wiley, 1994)
13. Dilution of Precision in GPS, http://en.wikipedia.org/wiki/Dilution_of_precision_%28GPS%29
14. D.G. Lowe, Object recognition from local scale-invariant features, in *ICCV* (1999)
15. H. Bay, A. Ess, T. Tuytelaars, L.V. Gool, Surf: speeded up robust features, in *Computer Vision and Image Understanding* (2008)
16. M.A. Fischler, R.C. Bolles, Random sample consensus: a paradigm for model fitting with applications to image analysis and automated cartography, in *CVIU* (2008)
17. S. Sahni, T. Gonzalez, P-complete approximation problems. J. ACM **23**(3), 555–565 (1976)
18. I. Constandache, X. Bao, M. Azizyan, R.R. Choudhury, Did you see bob?: human localization using mobile phones, in *ACM MobiCom* (2010)
19. M. Azizyan, I. Constandache, R.R. Choudhury, Surroundsense: mobile phone localization via ambience fingerprinting, in *ACM MobiCom* (2009)
20. H. Wang, S. Sen, A. Elgohary, M. Farid, M. Youssef, R.R. Choudhury, No need to war-drive: unsupervised indoor localization, in *ACM MobiSys* (2012), pp. 197–210
21. J. Manweiler, P. Jain, R.R. Choudhury, Satellites in our pockets: an object positioning system using smartphones, in *MobiSys* (2012), pp. 211–224
22. P. Robertson, M. Angermann, B. Krach, Simultaneous localization and mapping for pedestrians using only foot-mounted inertial sensors, in *ACM Ubicomp* (2009)
23. Z. Zhang, X. Zhou, W. Zhang, Y. Zhang, G. Wang, B.Y. Zhao, H. Zheng, I am the antenna: accurate outdoor ap location using smartphones, in *ACM MobiCom* (2011)
24. S. Sen, R.R. Choudhury, S. Nelakuditi, Spinloc: spin once to know your location, in *HotMobile* (2012)

Chapter 5
Smartphone-Based Real-Time Vehicle Tracking in Indoor Parking Structures

Abstract Although location awareness and turn-by-turn instructions are prevalent outdoors due to GPS, we are back into the darkness in uninstrumented indoor environments such as underground parking structures. We get confused, disoriented when driving in these mazes, and frequently forget where we parked, ending up circling back and forth upon return. In this chapter, we propose VeTrack, a smartphone-only system that tracks the vehicle's location in real time using the phone's inertial sensors. It does not require any environment instrumentation or cloud backend. It uses a novel "shadow" trajectory tracing method to accurately estimate phone's and vehicle's orientations despite their arbitrary poses and frequent disturbances. We develop algorithms in a Sequential Monte Carlo framework to represent vehicle states probabilistically, and harness constraints by the garage map and detected landmarks to robustly infer the vehicle location. We also find landmark (e.g., speed bumps and turns) recognition methods reliable against noises, disturbances from bumpy rides, and even handheld movements. We implement a highly efficient prototype and conduct extensive experiments in multiple parking structures of different sizes and structures, and collect data with multiple vehicles and drivers. We find that VeTrack can estimate the vehicle's real-time location with almost negligible latency, with error of $2 \sim 4$ parking spaces at the 80th percentile.

5.1 Introduction

Thanks to decades of efforts in GPS systems and devices, drivers know their locations at any time outdoors. The location awareness enables drivers to make proper decisions and gives them a sense of "control." However, whenever we drive into indoor environments such as underground parking garages, or multilevel parking structures where GPS signals can hardly penetrate, we lose this location awareness. Not only do we get confused, disoriented in maze-like structures, frequently we do not even remember where we park the car, ending up circling back and forth searching for the vehicle.

© The Author(s) 2018   81
R. Gao et al., *Smartphone-Based Indoor Map Construction*,
SpringerBriefs in Computer Science, https://doi.org/10.1007/978-981-10-8378-5_5

Providing real-time vehicle tracking capability indoors will satisfy the fundamental and constant cognitive needs of drivers to orient themselves relative to a large and unfamiliar environment. Knowing where they are generates a sense of control and induces calmness psychologically, both greatly enhancing the driving experience. In smart parking systems where free parking space information is available, real-time tracking will enable turn-by-turn instructions guiding drivers to those spaces, or at least areas where more spaces are likely available. The final parking location recorded can also be used to direct the driver back upon return, avoiding any back and forth search.

However, real-time vehicle tracking indoors is far from straightforward. First, mainstream indoor localization technology leverages RF signals such as WiFi [1, 2] and cellular [3], which can be sparse, intermittent or simply non-existent in many uninstrumented environments. Instrumenting the environment [4, 5] unfortunately is not always feasible: the acquisition, installation and maintenance of sensors require significant time, financial costs, and human efforts; simply wiring legacy environments can be a major undertaking. The lack of radio signals also means lack of Internet connectivity: no cloud service is reachable and all sensing/computing have to happen locally.

In this chapter, we propose VeTrack, a real-time vehicle tracking system that utilizes inertial sensors in the smartphone to provide accurate vehicle location. It does not rely on GPS/RF signals, or any additional sensors instrumenting the environment. All sensing and computation occur in the phone and no cloud backend is needed. A driver simply starts the VeTrack application before entering a parking structure, then VeTrack will track the vehicle movements, estimate and display its location in a garage map in real time, and record the final parking location, which can be used by the driver later to find the vehicle.

Such an inertial and phone-only solution entails a series of nontrivial challenges. First, many different scenarios exist for the phone *pose* (i.e., relative orientation between its coordinate system to that of the vehicle), which is needed to transform phone movements into vehicle movements. The phone may be placed in arbitrary positions—lying flat on a surface, slanted into a cup holder. The vehicle may drive on a non-horizontal, sloped surface; it may not go straight up or down the slope (e.g., slanted parking spaces). Furthermore, unpredictable human or road condition disturbances (e.g., moved together with the driver's pants' pockets, or picked up from a cupholder; speed bumps or jerky driving jolting the phone) may change the phone pose frequently. Despite all these different scenarios and disturbances, the phone's pose must be reliably and quickly estimated.

Second, due to the lack of periodic acceleration patterns like a person's walking [6–8], the traveling distance of a vehicle cannot be easily estimated. Although landmarks (e.g., speed bumps and turns) causing unique inertial data patterns can calibrate the location [9], distinguishing such patterns from other movements robustly (e.g., driver picking up and then laying down the phone) and recognizing them reliably despite different parking structures, vehicles and drivers remain open questions.

Finally, we have to balance the conflict between tracking accuracy and latency. Delaying the location determination allows more time for computation and sensing, thus higher tracking accuracy. However, this delay inevitably increases tracking latency, which adversely impacts real-time performance and user experience. How to develop efficient tracking algorithms to achieve both reasonable accuracy and acceptable latency, while using resources only on the phone, is another great challenge.

VeTrack consists of several components to deal with the above challenges to achieve accurate, real-time tracking. First, we propose a novel "*shadow*" trajectory tracing method that greatly simplifies phone pose estimation and vehicle movements computation. It can handle slopes and slanted driving on slopes; it is highly robust to inevitable noises and can quickly re-estimate the pose after each disturbance. We devise robust landmark detection algorithms that can reliably distinguish landmarks from disturbances (e.g., drivers picking up the phone) causing seemingly similar inertial patterns. Based on the vehicle movements and detected landmarks, we develop a highly robust yet efficient probabilistic framework to track a vehicle's location.

In summary, we make the following contributions:

- We develop a novel robust and efficient "shadow" trajectory tracing method. Unlike existing methods [10–12] that track the 3-axis relative angles between the phone and vehicle, it only tracks a single heading direction difference. To the best of our knowledge, it is the first that can handle slopes and slanted driving on slopes, and re-estimates a changed pose almost instantaneously.
- We design states and algorithms in a Sequential Monte Carlo framework that leverages constraints from garage maps and detected landmarks to reliably infer a vehicle's location. It uses probability distributions to represent a vehicle's states. We further propose a one-dimensional *road skeleton* model to reduce the vehicle state complexity, and a prediction–rollback mechanism to cut down tracking latency, both by one order of magnitude to enable real-time tracking.
- We propose robust landmark detection algorithms to recognize commonly encountered landmarks. They can reliably distinguish true landmarks from disturbances that exhibit similar inertial data patterns.
- We implement a prototype and conduct extensive experiments with different parking structures, vehicles, and drivers. We find that it can track the vehicle in real time against even disturbances such as drivers picking up the phone. It has almost negligible tracking latency, $10°$ pose and $2 \sim 4$ parking spaces' location errors at the 80th percentile, which are sufficient for most real-time driving and parked vehicle finding.

Next, we give a brief overview (Sect. 5.2), describe the shadow trajectory tracing (Sect. 5.3), sequential Monte Carlo algorithm design and the simplified road skeleton model (Sect. 5.4), and landmark detection algorithms and prediction–rollback

(Sect. 5.5). We report evaluation (Sect. 5.6) and discuss limitations (Sect. 5.7). After a review of related work (Sect. 5.8), we conclude the chapter.

5.2 Design Overview

VeTrack utilizes smartphone inertial data and garage floor maps (assumed already available) as inputs and simplifies the 3D vehicle tracing problem in the data transformation stage (Fig. 5.1). It leverages the probabilistic framework with landmark detection results and prediction/rollback mechanism for robust and real-time tracking.

The data transformation stage contains two components, i.e., shadow trajectory tracing and road skeleton model. Shadow trajectory tracing tracks the vehicle's shadow's movements on 2D plane instead of the vehicle in 3D space; the road skeleton model abstracts 2D strip roads into 1D line segments to remove inconsequential details while keeping the basic shape and topology. They together simplify the 3D vehicle tracing problem into 1D.

To deal with noises and disturbances in data, VeTrack explicitly represents the states of vehicles (e.g., locations) with probabilities and we develop algorithms in a Sequential Monte Carlo framework for robust tracking. We also leverage landmark detection results to help calibrate the vehicle locations to where such landmarks exist, and the prediction/rollback mechanism to generate instantaneous landmark recognition results while the vehicle has only partially passed landmarks.

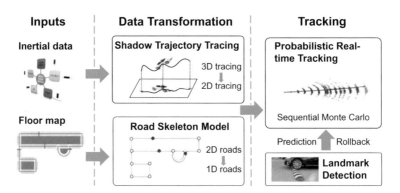

Fig. 5.1 In data transformation stage, the shadow trajectory tracing simplifies 3D vehicle tracing into 2D shadow tracing while road skeleton model further reduces 2D tracing into 1D. In tracking stage, VeTrack represents vehicle states probabilistically and uses a Sequential Monte Carlo framework for robust tracking. It also uses landmark detection to calibrate vehicle states and prediction/rollback for minimum latency

5.3 Trajectory Tracing

5.3.1 Conventional Approaches

Inferring a vehicle's location via smartphone inertial sensors is not trivial. Naive methods such as double integration of 3D accelerations ($\overrightarrow{x}(t) = \iint \overrightarrow{a}(t)dt$) generate chaotic 3D trajectories due to the noisy inertial sensors. Below we list two conventional approaches.

Method 1: Motion transformation. It is a straightforward approach that transforms the motion information (i.e., acceleration and orientation) from a phone to a vehicle, and eventually to that in the global 2D coordinate system. This requires the vehicle's acceleration in the global coordinate system G be estimated. After measuring the phone's acceleration from inertial sensors, existing work [10–12] usually takes a three-step approach to transform it into vehicle's acceleration.

Assume the three axes of the vehicle's coordinate system are X^V, Y^V, and Z^V. First, the gravity direction is obtained using mobile OS APIs [13] that use low-pass Butterworth filters to remove high-frequency components caused by rotation and translation movements [14]. It is assumed to be the direction of Z^V in the phone's coordinate system (i.e., vehicles moving on level ground).

Next, the gravity direction component is deducted to obtain the acceleration on the horizontal plane. The direction of maximum acceleration (caused by vehicle accelerating or decelerating) is estimated as Y^V (i.e., forward direction). Finally, X^V is determined as the cross product of Y^V and Z^V using the right-hand rule. The X^V, Y^V, and Z^V directions in the phone's coordinate system give a transformation matrix that converts the phone's acceleration into that of the vehicle.

Figure 5.2a shows the result of tracing a vehicle on a straight road via motion transformation. During investigation, we find several limitations. First, when a vehicle is on a slope (straight up/down or slanted), the direction of gravity is no longer the Z-axis of the vehicle. Second, accelerometers are highly noisy and susceptible to various disturbances from driving dynamics and road conditions. Thus, the direction of the maximum horizontal acceleration may not always be the Y-axis. In experiments, we find that it has around 40° errors at the 80th percentile. Finally, to reliably detect the direction of maximum horizontal acceleration, a changed phone pose must remain the same at least 4 s [12], which may be impossible when frequent disturbances exist.

Method 2: 3D trajectory tracing. Instead of direct double integrating on the original acceleration vector ($\overrightarrow{x}(t) = \iint \overrightarrow{a}(t)dt$), it uses the moving direction of the vehicle (unit length vector $\overrightarrow{T}(t)$) and its speed amplitude $s(t)$: $\overrightarrow{x}(t) = \int \overrightarrow{T}(t) \cdot s(t)dt$, where $s(t)$ can be computed as $\int a(t)dt$, integration of the acceleration amplitude along moving direction. Although there are still two integrations, the impact of vertical direction noises is eliminated due to the projection, and the moving direction $\overrightarrow{T}(t)$ can be measured reliably by gyroscope.

Figure 5.2b shows the result for 3D trajectory tracing. We observe that it obtains better orientation accuracy than motion transformation, i.e., 3° errors of the example trace, but it assumes fixed phone pose in car. In addition, raw gyroscope readings suffer linear drifts [14] and reach 32° angle errors after an 8-minute driving in our measurements.

5.3.2   Shadow Trajectory Tracing

To overcome the above limitations, we propose a "shadow" trajectory tracing method that traces the movement of the vehicle's *shadow* projected onto the 2D horizontal plane (Fig. 5.3a). Points O and O' represent the positions of the vehicle and its shadow. $\overrightarrow{OV}$ and $\overrightarrow{OA}$ are the velocity and acceleration of the vehicle in 3D space. V' and A' are the projection of V and A onto the 2D ground. It can be shown easily that $\overrightarrow{O'V'}$ and $\overrightarrow{O'A'}$ are the velocity and acceleration of the shadow. This is simply because the projection eliminates the vertical direction component but preserves those on the horizontal plane, thus the shadow and vehicle have the same horizontal acceleration, and thus the same 2D plane velocity and coordinates.

Shadow tracing algorithm: We need to estimate three variables in this method (Fig. 5.3b): (1) the shadow's moving direction $\overrightarrow{O'V'}$ (i.e., $\overrightarrow{T}(t)$) in the global coordinate system. (2) the horizontal (i.e., shadow's) acceleration $\overrightarrow{O'A'}$. (3) angle $\angle V'O'A'$ ($\angle 1$), the angle between the horizontal acceleration vector and vehicle's shadow's heading (i.e., moving) direction; this is used to project the shadow's acceleration along the vehicle moving direction $\overrightarrow{O'V'}$ to get tangential acceleration amplitude $|\overrightarrow{O'A''}|$ (i.e., $s(t)$).

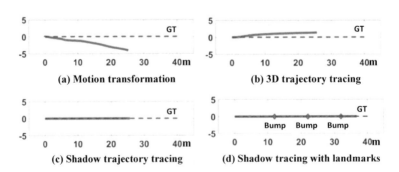

Fig. 5.2 Illustration of vehicle tracing using different methods: **a** motion transformation; **b** 3D trajectory tracing with gyroscope; **c** shadow trajectory tracing; **d** shadow trajectory tracing with landmarks

Next, we explain how to estimate them in three steps.

(1) When the vehicle is driving straight, the shadow's moving direction is approximated by the direction of the road, which can be obtained from the garage map and the current location estimation. When the vehicle is turning around a corner, VeTrack accumulates the gyroscope's "yaw" (around gravity direction) to modify the heading direction until the vehicle goes straight again. We develop robust algorithms to distinguish straight driving from turning and disturbances (Sect. 5.5).

(2) From existing mobile OS APIs [13], the gravity direction can be detected. We deduct the gravity direction component from the phone's acceleration vector to obtain the horizontal acceleration vector $\overrightarrow{O'A'}$.

(3) Figure 5.3b illustrates how to calculate $\angle 1$ ($\angle V'O'A'$): $\angle 1 = \angle 2 + \angle 3 - \angle 4$ (i.e., $\angle V'O'A' = \angle GO'P' + \angle P'O'A' - \angle GO'V'$). $\overrightarrow{O'G}, \overrightarrow{O'P'}, \overrightarrow{O'V'}$ are the Y-axes of the global, phone's shadow's and vehicle's shadow's coordinate system. (3.1) $\angle 2$ is the phone's shadow's heading direction in the global coordinate system. Its relative changes can be obtained reliably from the gyroscope's "yaw", and we use a distribution around the compass' reading upon entering the garage to initialize it. Because the Sequential Monte Carlo framework can calibrate and quickly reduce the error (Sect. 5.4), an accurate initial direction is not necessary. (3.2) $\angle 3$ is essentially the horizontal acceleration direction in the phone's shadow's coordinate system, which is already obtained in step 2. (3.3) $\angle 4$ is the vehicle's shadow's moving direction in the global coordinate system, already obtained in step 1.

Observation: Figure 5.2c shows the result for shadow trajectory tracing. We observe that the vehicle's moving direction is measured reliably by the map (i.e., forward/backward along pathways only) while phone's short-time movement in car is monitored by gyroscope, thus our method achieves better angle accuracy and robustness than the conventional approaches. However, vehicle's distance error is still larger than 14 m due to noisy accelerometer on smartphone, thus we identify landmarks (three bumps in Fig. 5.2d) to calibrate the vehicle's position. From the combination of shadow tracing and landmark calibration, the vehicle's position error is 3 m with no angle error.

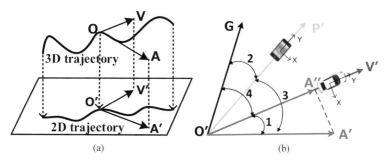

(a)   (b)

Fig. 5.3 a Intuition: points O and O' are the positions of vehicle and its shadow. $\overrightarrow{OV}$ and $\overrightarrow{OA}$ are the velocity and acceleration of vehicle in the 3D space. V' and A' are the projection of V and A onto the 2D ground. **b** Illustration of the method to estimate $\angle 1$ from $\angle 2$, $\angle 3$, and $\angle 4$

5.3.3 Equivalence Proof

Here, we regard the 3D trajectory tracing method as the baseline, and prove that our shadow trajectory tracing method is equivalent to it in most cases and with only a small bounded difference in other cases. Note that the theoretical model and proof provide more confidence about the applicability of our approach, and a way to validate if it can be applied in certain environments.

Modeling. We denote the notations as follows. Assume P and V are the phone's and vehicle's local coordinate systems, G the global one. When used as superscripts, they denote in which coordinate system a variable is defined. V' is the vehicle's local coordinate system V rotated such that the XY-plane become horizontal,[1] and the 3×3 transformation matrix from coordinate system C_1 to C_2 as $\boldsymbol{R}_{C_1}^{C_2}$. Also, two projection matrices will be used, $\boldsymbol{E}_1 = \mathrm{diag}([0, 1, 1])$ and $\boldsymbol{E}_3 = \mathrm{diag}([1, 1, 0])$ where $\mathrm{diag}(\cdot)$ represents a diagonal square matrix with the specified elements on the diagonal.

(1) Baseline: 3D trajectory tracing. First, we convert the phone's acceleration in its coordinate system P into that in the vehicle's coordinate system V, i.e., $a_0^P \rightarrow a_0^V$ (shown on the left part in Fig. 5.4), and then extract the tangential acceleration (i.e., acceleration along the vehicle's instantaneous moving direction) which will be transformed into the global coordinate system and integrated over time for speed and thus 3D trajectory. The pipeline of 3D trajectory tracing method has four stages:

1. $\boldsymbol{a}_0^P$, phone's acceleration in P.
2. $\boldsymbol{a}_0^V = \boldsymbol{R}_P^V \boldsymbol{a}_0^P$, vehicle's acceleration in V.
3. $\boldsymbol{a}_1^V = \boldsymbol{E}_1 \boldsymbol{a}_0^V$, vehicle's tangential acceleration after eliminating radial acceleration.
4. $\boldsymbol{a}_1^G = \boldsymbol{R}_V^G \boldsymbol{a}_1^V$, vehicle's tangential acceleration in G.

Let $\Gamma(t)$ denote the projection of vehicle's tangential acceleration on horizontal plane at time t, which can be represented as

$$\Gamma(t) = \boldsymbol{E}_3 \boldsymbol{R}_V^G(t) \boldsymbol{E}_1 \boldsymbol{R}_P^V(t) \boldsymbol{a}_0^P(t), \tag{5.1}$$

where $\boldsymbol{E}_3$ is the projection.

(2) Our shadow trajectory tracing method simply tracks the vehicle's shadow on horizontal plane, and its process has five steps (shown on the right part in Fig. 5.4):

1. $\boldsymbol{a}_0^P$, phone's acceleration in P.
2. $\boldsymbol{a}_0^{V'} = \boldsymbol{R}_P^{V'} \boldsymbol{a}_0^P$, vehicle shadow's acceleration in V'.
3. $\boldsymbol{a}_1^{V'} = \boldsymbol{E}_3 \boldsymbol{a}_0^{V'}$, vehicle shadow's horizontal acceleration in V'.
4. $\boldsymbol{a}_2^{V'} = \boldsymbol{E}_1 \boldsymbol{a}_1^{V'}$, vehicle shadow's tangential acceleration in V'.
5. $\boldsymbol{a}_2^G = \boldsymbol{R}_{V'}^G \boldsymbol{a}_2^{V'}$, vehicle shadow's tangential acceleration in G.

---

[1] This is done by pitching X-axis horizontal then Y-axis horizontal.

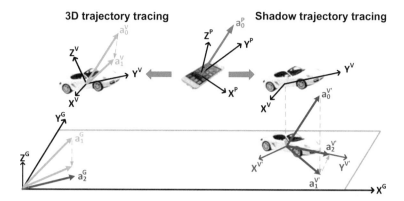

Fig. 5.4 Illustration of 3D trajectory tracing and shadow trajectory tracing. Left part: 3D trajectory tracing, $a_0^P \rightarrow a_0^V \rightarrow a_1^V \rightarrow a_1^G$; right part: shadow trajectory tracing, $a_0^P \rightarrow a_0^{V'} \rightarrow a_1^{V'} \rightarrow a_2^{V'} \rightarrow a_2^G$

Similarly, we denote $\Delta(t)$ as the shadow's tangential acceleration on horizontal plane, which is computed as

$$\Delta(t) = R_{V'}^G(t) E_1 E_3 R_P^{V'}(t) a_0^P(t). \tag{5.2}$$

Theorem: The baseline 3D trajectory tracing method and our shadow trajectory tracing method are equivalent when the X-axis or Y-axis of the vehicle (X^V or Y^V) is horizontal. Otherwise, their tangential accelerations' difference is bounded by vehicle's radial acceleration times $\frac{sin^2\phi}{1+cos\phi}$, i.e.,

$$|\Gamma(t) - \Delta(t)| \leq \frac{sin^2\phi}{1 + cos\phi} \cdot |a_0^v - a_1^v|,$$

where ϕ is the inclination angle of the slope.

We prove some Lemmas before proving the theorem.

Lemma 5.1 E_1 and E_3 are commutable.

Proof Diagonal matrices are commutable.

Lemma 5.2 E_3 is commutable with $R_{V'}^G(t)$.

Proof $R_{V'}^G(t)$ is degenerated rotation along the Z-axis (Z^G and $Z^{V'}$). Thus, it is commutable with E_3 which eliminates the Z-axis component.

Lemma 5.3 E_1 and $R_{V'}^V(t)$ are commutable when the X-axis or Y-axis of the vehicle is horizontal, otherwise $|\Gamma(t) - \Delta(t)| \leq \frac{sin^2\phi}{1+cos\phi} \cdot a_n$, where ϕ is the inclination angle of the slope and a_n is the vehicle's radial acceleration.

Proof As shown in Fig. 5.5a, we assume the vehicle O is moving on a slope (tangent plane) with inclination angle of ϕ, and its heading direction at angle θ to the direction of slope. $a = (a_t, a_n) = (|\overrightarrow{OT}|, |\overrightarrow{ON}|)$ are the vehicle's tangential and radial accelerations.

Next, we build the spatial and plane geometry models for the two tracing methods (shown in Fig. 5.5b, c). In 3D trajectory tracing, the vehicle's tangential acceleration on horizontal plane is calculated as $\overrightarrow{OT'}$; while in shadow trajectory tracing, it is computed as $\overrightarrow{OT'} + \overrightarrow{ON''}$ where N'' denotes the projection of N' onto line $\overrightarrow{OT'}$ (the direction of vehicle's shadow). The cause of their difference $\overrightarrow{ON''}$ is that the projection of a right angle ($\angle TON$) onto horizontal ground is no longer a right angle ($\angle T'ON' = \delta$), and thus vehicle's radial acceleration $\overrightarrow{ON}$ also produces horizontal acceleration component.

Then, we compute their difference value $\overrightarrow{ON''}$. From Fig. 5.5b, we count that $|OL| = a_n \cos\theta$, $|OR| = a_t \sin\theta$, $|LN'| = a_n \sin\theta \cos\phi$, $|RT'| = a_t \cos\theta \cos\phi$. Thus, $\overrightarrow{ON''}$ in Fig. 5.5c can be computed via the cosine theorem:

$$\overrightarrow{ON''} = |ON'| \cos\delta = \frac{-a_n \sin\theta \sin^2\phi}{\sqrt{\cos^2\phi + \tan^2\theta}} \tag{5.3}$$

From Eq. 5.3, we observe that the difference between two tracing methods does not rely on the vehicle's tangential acceleration, and they have no differences when the vehicle drives on horizontal plane ($\phi = 0°$), or either of X-, Y-axis of the vehicle is horizontal ($\theta = 0°$ or $90°$).

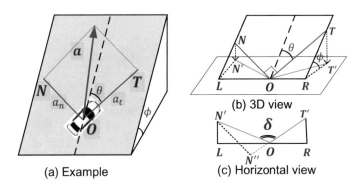

(a) Example   (b) 3D view   (c) Horizontal view

Fig. 5.5 **a** Driving a vehicle O on the slope with acceleration a; **b** 3D view, the inclination angle of slope is ϕ, and vehicle's heading direction $\overrightarrow{OT}$ is at angle θ to the direction of slope; **c** horizontal plane view

Furthermore, we leverage algebraic formulas to compute the maximum value of $|\overrightarrow{ON''}|$, i.e., the bound of difference between two tracing methods. Given a fixed slope with inclination angle of ϕ, the maximum value of $|\overrightarrow{ON''}|$ is computed as

$$|\overrightarrow{ON''}| = \frac{a_n \sin^2 \phi}{\sqrt{\frac{\cos^2 \phi}{\sin^2 \theta} + \frac{1}{\cos^2 \theta}}} \leq \frac{\sin^2 \phi}{1 + \cos \phi} \cdot a_n \qquad (5.4)$$

and its maximum value is obtained when $\theta = \arcsin \sqrt{\frac{\cos \phi}{1 + \cos \phi}}$.

Thus, when the X-axis or Y-axis of the vehicle is horizontal, two tracing methods are equivalent and $R_{V'}^V(\tau)$ is degenerated rotation along X-axis or Y-axis thus commutable with matrix E_1, which is similar to the case in Lemma 5.2.

Otherwise, those two matrices are not commutable since projections of two perpendicular lines to horizontal plane are no longer perpendicular. However, the difference is bounded based on the inclination angle of the slope. Most garage paths have small degrees of slope, if any. For example, for $10°$ and $20°$ slopes, the difference between two tracing methods is less than 2 and 7% of vehicle's radial acceleration, respectively.

Now we prove the theorem, i.e., the equivalence between $\Gamma(t)$ in 3D trajectory tracing and $\Delta(t)$ in shadow trajectory tracing when X-axis or Y-axis of the vehicle is horizontal.

Proof When X-axis or Y-axis of the vehicle is horizontal,

$$\begin{aligned}
\Delta(t) &= R_{V'}^G(t) E_1 E_3 R_P^{V'}(t) a_0^P(t) \text{(Eq. 5.2)} \\
&= R_{V'}^G(t) E_3 E_1 R_P^{V'}(t) a_0^P(t) \text{(Lemma 5.1)} \\
&= E_3 R_{V'}^G(t) E_1 R_P^{V'}(t) a_0^P(t) \text{(Lemma 5.2)} \\
&= E_3 R_V^G(t) R_{V'}^V(t) E_1 R_P^{V'}(t) a_0^P(t) \\
&= E_3 R_V^G(t) E_1 R_{V'}^V(t) R_P^{V'}(t) a_0^P(t) \text{(Lemma 5.3)} \\
&= E_3 R_V^G(t) E_1 R_P^V(t) a_0^P(t) = \Gamma(t) \text{(Eq. 5.1)}
\end{aligned} \qquad (5.5)$$

Thus, $\Gamma(t)$ in 3D trajectory tracing and $\Delta(t)$ in shadow trajectory tracing are equivalent in this case.

Comparison: Despite their equivalence in most cases, shadow tracing needs much less variables and is subject to less noises, thus more robust than 3D tracing. (1) Shadow tracing does not need to track variables in the vertical dimension (e.g., altitude, angle, speed, and acceleration). All of them are subject to noises and require more complexity to estimate. (2) On the horizontal plane, the moving direction can be estimated accurately based on the prior knowledge of road directions (Sect. 5.4.4). The distance is computed using the acceleration amplitude along the moving direction. Thus, inertial noises perpendicular to the moving direction do not impact the distance estimation. (3) Shadow tracing uses gyroscopes to estimate pose, while conventional approaches use accelerometers that are more susceptible to external disturbances. Therefore, shadow tracing is much less complex, subject to less noises, and thus achieves better accuracy and higher robustness.

During experiments, we find that our shadow tracing method can handle arbitrary phone and vehicle poses and the vehicle can go straight up/down or slanted on a slope. It has much smaller errors ($5 \sim 10°$ at the 80th percentile) and better robustness. It also re-estimates a changed phone pose almost instantaneously because gyroscopes have little latency; thus, it can handle frequent disturbances.

5.4 Real-Time Tracking

5.4.1 Intuition

The basic idea to locate the vehicle is to leverage two types of constraints imposed by the map, namely paths and landmarks. Given a trajectory estimated from inertial data (Fig. 5.6), there are only a few paths on the map that can accommodate the trajectory. Each detected landmark (e.g., a speed bump or turn) can pinpoint the vehicle to a few possible locations. Jointly considering the two constraints can further reduce the uncertainty and limit the possible placement of the trajectory, thus revealing the vehicle location. We will first describe the tracking design here, and then landmark detection in Sect. 5.5.

To achieve robust and real-time tracking, we need to address a dual challenge. First, the inertial data have significant noises and disturbances. Smartphones do not possess a speedometer or odometer to directly measure the velocity or distance; they are obtained from acceleration integration, which is known to generate cubic error accumulation [9]. External disturbances (e.g., handheld movements or road conditions) cause sudden and drastic changes to vehicle movements. Together they make it impossible to obtain accurate trajectories from inertial data only. Second,

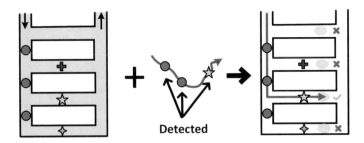

Fig. 5.6 Using both map constraints and detected landmarks can narrow down the possible placement of the trajectory more quickly

the requirement of low latency tracking demands efficient algorithms that can run on resource-limited phones. We have to minimize computational complexity so no cloud backend is needed.

To achieve robustness, we use probability distributions to explicitly represent vehicle states (e.g., location and speed) and the sequential Monte Carlo (SMC) method to maintain the states. This is inspired by probabilistic robotics [15]: instead of a single "best guess", the probability distributions cover the whole space of possible hypotheses about vehicle locations, and use evidences from sensing data to validate the likelihoods of these hypotheses. This results in much better robustness to noises in data. To achieve efficiency, we use a 1D "*road skeleton*" model that abstracts paths into one-dimensional line segments. We find this dramatically reduces the size of vehicle states. Thus, the number of hypotheses is cut by almost one order of magnitude, which is critical to achieve real-time tracking on resource-limited phones. Next, we will describe the road skeleton model and the detailed SMC design.

5.4.2 Road Skeleton Model

The road skeleton model greatly simplifies the representation of garage maps. It abstracts away inconsequential details and keeps only the essential aspects important to tracking. Thus, it helps reduce computational overheads in the probabilistic framework. We assume that garage maps are available (e.g., from operators), while how to construct them is beyond the scope of this book.

Given a map of the 3D multilevel parking structure, we represent each level by projecting its map onto a 2D horizontal plane perpendicular to the gravity direction. Thus, the vehicle location can be represented by a number indicating the current level, and a 2D coordinate for its location on this level. To accommodate changes when a vehicle moves across adjacent levels, we introduce "virtual boundaries" in the middle of the ramp connecting two levels. As shown in Fig. 5.7b, a vehicle crossing the dash line of the virtual boundary between levels will be assigned a different level number. This kind of 2D representation suits the needs for shadow tracing while retaining the essential topology and shape for tracking.

Note that we call it 2D representation because the floor level remains unchanged and does not need detection most of the time. It is updated only when the vehicle crosses virtual boundaries between levels. Its estimation is also much simpler and easier than accurate 2D tracking, where most challenges exist.

The key insight for the skeleton model is that the road width is not necessary for tracking vehicle locations. Since the paths are usually narrow enough for only one vehicle in each direction, the vehicle location has little freedom in the width direction. Thus, we simplify the road representation with their medial axis, and roads become 1D line segments without any width.

We have tried several geometrical algorithms to extract the road skeleton from garage floor map. A naive method is to extract the road boundary, then leverage Voronoi diagram [16] to generate the middle line inside the road boundary (shown

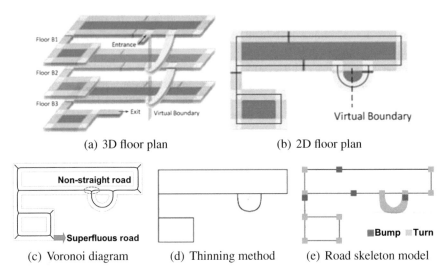

(a) 3D floor plan   (b) 2D floor plan

(c) Voronoi diagram   (d) Thinning method   (e) Road skeleton model

Fig. 5.7 **a** shows the 3D floor plans of a multilevel parking structure. A vehicle enters the entrance on the floor B1 and goes down to other two levels crossing the virtual boundaries. **b** shows the 2D projection of Floor B2 in (**a**). **c** shows the road skeleton via Voronoi diagram, and there are superfluous and non-straight 1D lines. Trajectory tracing shows the road skeleton via a robust thinning method. **e** shows the final 1D road skeleton model, with points representing landmarks (corresponding to bumps and turns)

in Fig. 5.7c). However, we observe that there are superfluous and deformed, non-straight 1D line segments on the skeleton. Those mistakes are difficult to remove by simple geometrical algorithms.

Thus, we leverage a robust thinning method [17] to extract the road skeleton (Fig. 5.7d) and eliminate such problems. Then, we project the bumps from garage floor map onto the road skeleton and use a 3×3 pixel template to find road turns on the skeleton map. The final road skeleton model with landmarks is shown in Fig. 5.7e.

Compared to a straightforward 2D strip representation of roads, the skeleton model reduces the freedom of vehicle location by one dimension, thus greatly cutting down the state space size in the probabilistic framework and resulting in one order of magnitude less complexity.

5.4.3   *Probabilistic Tracking Framework*

The tracking problem is formulated as a sequential Monte Carlo (SMC) problem, specifically, the particle filtering framework [15]. The vehicle states (e.g., location, speed) at time t are represented by a multidimensional random variable $s(t)$. Each hypothesis (with concrete values for each dimension of $s(t)$) is called a "particle" and a collection of J particles $\{s_t^{(j)}\}_{j=1}^J$ are used to represent the distribution of possible vehicle states at time t.

The framework operates on discrete time $\{1, ..., t-1, t, ...\}$ and repeats three steps for each time slot. Without loss of generality, we assume J particles $\{s_{t-1}^{(j)}\}_{j=1}^J$ already exist at $t-1$ and describe the progress from $t-1$ to t.

State update predicts the set of states $\{\hat{s}_t^{(j)}\}_{j=1}^J$ at time t based on two known inputs, the previous state $\{s_{t-1}^{(j)}\}_{j=1}^J$ and most recent movement m_t such as the speed, acceleration that govern the movement of the vehicle. For example, given the previous location and most recent speed, one can predict a vehicle's next location. To capture uncertainties in movement and previous states, a random noise is added to the estimated location. Thus, J predictions $\{\hat{s}_t^{(j)}\}_{j=1}^J$ are generated.

Weight update uses measurements z_t made at time t to examine how much evidence exists for each prediction, so as to adjust the weights of particles $\{\hat{s}_t^{(j)}\}_{j=1}^J$. The likelihood $p(z_t|s_t)$, how likely the measurement z_t would happen given state s_t, is the evidence. A prediction $\hat{s}_t^{(j)}$ with a higher likelihood $p(z_t|s_t = \hat{s}_t^{(j)})$ will receive a proportionally higher weight $w_t^{(j)} = w_{t-1}^{(j)} p(z_t|s_t = \hat{s}_t^{(j)})$. Then, all weights are normalized to ensure that $\{w_t^{(j)}\}_{j=1}^J$ sum to 1.

Resampling draws J particles from the current state prediction set $\{\hat{s}_t^{(j)}\}_{j=1}^J$ with probabilities proportional to their weights $\{w_t^{(j)}\}_{j=1}^J$, thus creating the new state set $\{s_t^{(j)}\}_{j=1}^J$ to replace the old set $\{s_{t-1}^{(j)}\}_{j=1}^J$. Then, the next iteration starts.

Note that the above is only a framework. The critical task is the detailed design of particle states, update, and resampling procedures. Thus, we cannot simply copy what has been done in related work, and have to carefully design algorithms tailored to our specific problem.

5.4.4 Tracking Algorithms

State and Initialization

Our particle state is a collection of factors that can impact the vehicle tracking. Since the number of particles grows exponentially with the dimensionality of the state, we select most related factors to reduce the complexity while still preserving tracking accuracy. Our particle states include

- level number k,
- position on 2D floor plane $X = (x, y)$,
- speed of the vehicle v, and
- α/β, phone/vehicle shadows' 2D heading directions.

The first dimension k is introduced for multilevel structures. Position of the vehicle is represented as a 2D coordinate $X = (x, y)$ for convenience. In reality, due to the

1D skeleton road model, the position actually has only one degree of freedom. This greatly reduces the number of particles needed.

Initialization of particles: We use certain prior knowledge to initialize the particles' state. The last GPS location before entering the parking structure is used to infer the entrance, thus the level number k and 2D entrance location (x, y). The vehicle speed v is assumed to start from zero. The vehicle heading direction β is approximated by the direction of the entrance path segment, and the phone heading direction α is drawn from a distribution based on the compass reading before entering the garage. As shown later (Sect. 5.6), the phone's heading direction can be calibrated to within $15°$, showing strong robustness against compass errors known to be nontrivial [18].

State Update

For a particle with state $(k_{t-1}, x_{t-1}, y_{t-1}, v_{t-1}, \alpha_{t-1}, \beta_{t-1})$, we create a prediction $(\hat{k}_t, \hat{x}_t, \hat{y}_t, \hat{v}_t, \hat{\alpha}_t, \hat{\beta}_t)$ given movement $m_t = (a_x, a_y, \omega_z)$ where $a_x, a_y,$ and ω_z are X-, Y-axis accelerations and Z-axis angular speed in the coordinate system of the phone's shadow.

First, $(\hat{x}_t, \hat{y}_t)$ is updated as follows:

$$\hat{x}_t = x_{t-1} + v_{t-1} \Delta t \cdot \cos \beta_{t-1} + \varepsilon_x, \tag{5.6}$$

$$\hat{y}_t = y_{t-1} + v_{t-1} \Delta t \cdot \sin \beta_{t-1} + \varepsilon_y, \tag{5.7}$$

where $\varepsilon_x, \varepsilon_y$ are Gaussian noises. If $(\hat{x}_t, \hat{y}_t)$ is no longer on the skeleton, we project it back to the skeleton. Level number $\hat{k}_t$ is updated when a particle passes through a virtual boundary around the floor-connecting-ramp, otherwise $\hat{k}_t = k_{t-1}$.

Next, velocity v_t is updated as follows:

$$\hat{a}_t = a_y \cdot \cos \gamma_t - a_x \cdot \sin \gamma_t + \varepsilon_a, \tag{5.8}$$

$$\hat{v}_t = v_{t-1} + a_t \cdot \Delta t + \varepsilon_v, \tag{5.9}$$

where γ_t is the angle between the Y-axes of the two shadows' coordinate systems and $\varepsilon_a, \varepsilon_v$ are Gaussian noises.

Finally, α_t and β_t are updated as follows:

$$\hat{\alpha}_t = \alpha_{t-1} + \omega_z \Delta t + \varepsilon_\alpha, \tag{5.10}$$

$$\hat{\beta}_t = \begin{cases} \beta_{t-1} + \omega_z \Delta t + \varepsilon_\beta, & \text{if } turn = True; \\ \text{road direction at } (k_t, x_t, y_t), & \text{otherwise}, \end{cases} \tag{5.11}$$

where ε_α, ε_β are random Gaussian noises. The above allows the phone to change its angle α to accommodate occasional handheld or jolting movements, while such movements will not alter the vehicle's angle β if the vehicle is known to travel straight.

Weight Update

Weight update uses detected landmarks and floor plan constraints to recalculate the "importance" of the current particle states. The basic idea is to penalize particles that behave inconsistently given the floor plan constraints. For example, since a vehicle cannot travel perpendicularly to path direction, a particle with velocity orthogonal to the road direction will be penalized. It will have much smaller weights and less likely to be drawn during resampling.

We compute the weight w_t as

$$w_t := w_{t-1} \prod_{i=0}^{2} w_{ti}, \tag{5.12}$$

Each w_{ti} is described as follows.

- **Constraints imposed by the map**. We define $w_{t0} = \cos^2(\beta_t - \beta_{t-1})$. It is designed to penalize particles that have a drastic change in the vehicle heading direction, since during most of the time a vehicle does not make dramatic turns.
- **Detected landmarks**. When an i-th type landmark[2] is detected, w_{ti} of the current state is updated as $\mathcal{N}(D_i(x_t, y_t); 0, \sigma_i^2)$ where $D_i(x_t, y_t)$ is the distance to the closest landmark of the same type and σ_i^2 is a parameter controlling the scale of the distance. If no landmark is detected, $w_{ti} = 1$. This method penalizes the predicted states far away from detected landmarks.

Finally, all weights are normalized, so they sum up to 1.

Resampling

A replacement particle is selected from the predicted particle set $\{\hat{s}_t^{(j)}\}_{j=1}^{J}$ where each particle $\hat{s}_t^{(j)}$ has probability $w_t^{(j)}$ being selected. This is repeated for J times and J particles are selected to form the new state set $\{s_t^{(j)}\}_{j=1}^{J}$. Then, the next iteration starts.

---

[2]We use only bump and corner here because their locations are precise; turns are used in vehicle angle β update in Eq. 5.11.

5.5   Landmark Detection

A parking structure usually has a limited number of landmarks (e.g., speed bumps and turns), and their locations can be marked on the garage map. When a vehicle passes over a landmark, it causes distinctive inertial data patterns, which can be recognized to calibrate the vehicle's location.

However, realizing accurate and real-time landmark detection is not trivial because (1) road conditions and hand movements impose disturbances on inertial sensor readings; and (2) to minimize delay, landmark recognition results are needed based on partial data before the vehicle completely passes a landmark. We present landmark detection algorithms robust to noises and hand movements, and a prediction and rollback mechanism for instantaneous landmark detection.

5.5.1   Types of Landmarks

Speed bumps generate jolts, hence acceleration fluctuations in the Z-axis when a vehicle passes over. Note that drainage trench covers, fire shutter bottom supports may also cause similar jolting patterns. We include them as "bumps" as well in the garage map.

Many factors can cause ambiguities in bump detection. For example, Fig. 5.8 shows the acceleration signal along the Z-axis as a vehicle starts and passes over four bumps along a straight road. The first tremor in the left green box (around $10 \sim 17$ s marked with "J") is caused by the vehicle's starting acceleration. It lasts longer but with smaller magnitude compared to those caused by the bumps (in red boxes marked "$B1$"–"$B4$"). The tremor in the right green box (around 60 s marked "M") is due to the user's action—holding the phone in hand, and then uplifting the phone to check the location. They generate vertical acceleration that may be confused with those by bumps.

Turns are defined as durations in which a vehicle continuously changes its driving direction, usually around road corners. They can be detected from the gyroscope readings of angular velocities around the gravity direction (i.e., "yaw"). During turns, a vehicle's direction differs from the road direction. Its direction changes in such periods are accumulated to track the vehicle's heading direction.

There exists work [12] using simple thresholding on turning angles to detect turns. However, we find they cannot reliably distinguish vehicle turns from hand movements (e.g., putting the phone on adjacent seat and picking it up to check the location).

Corners. A turn may span over an extended period, from its start to the end. The corner where two road segments join can be used to precisely calibrate the vehicle's location. The main challenge is consecutive turns: they might be detected as a single one, hence missing some corners. For example, in Fig. 5.9a, the first two turns may be detected as only one turn period.

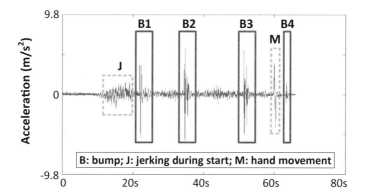

Fig. 5.8 Acceleration along the Z-axis. There are starting acceleration (J), four bumps (B1–B4), and one hand movement (M) along the trajectory

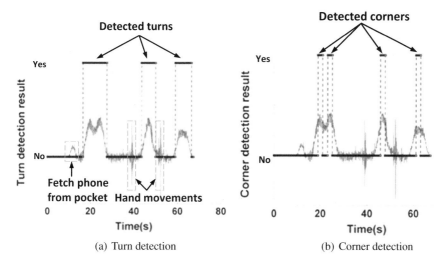

(a) Turn detection   (b) Corner detection

Fig. 5.9 Turn and corner detection. **a** Three turn periods are correctly detected, even there are several different hand movements. **b** Four corners are correctly separated, even when only three turned are detected

We observe that when a vehicle passes at a corner, its angular velocity usually is at a local maxima, corresponding to the maximum turn of the steering wheel. To identify corners precisely, we use a sliding window to find local maxima of angular velocities within each turning period. Each local maxima is marked as a corner. Figure 5.9b shows that the leftmost two consecutive corners within the same turn period are properly separated.

5.5.2 Feature and Classification Algorithm

We use machine learning techniques to recognize bumps and turns. Corners are detected within turns using the above local maxima searching. The critical issue is what features should be used. Although one may feed the raw signal directly to these algorithms, it is usually much more efficient to design succinct, distinctive features from raw signals.

For bumps, we divide acceleration along the Z-axis into 2-second windows sliding at 0.2 s intervals. This window size is chosen empirically such that both front and rear wheels can cross the bump for complete bump passing. For turns, we use gyroscope angular velocities around the vertical direction and divide the signal the same way. We observe that smaller windows lead to drastic accuracy drop, while larger ones incur more delay.

We observe that there are two kinds of common hand movements that may be confused with bumps or turns: (1) hold the phone in hand, and occasionally uplift it to check the location; (2) put the phone in pockets/nearby seat, pick up the phone to check the location, and then lay it down. The first causes a jitter in Z-axis acceleration and might be confused with bumps; the second also has Z-axis gyroscope changes and might be confused with turns.

We have tried a number of different feature designs, both time-domain and frequency-domain, to help distinguish such ambiguities. We list five feature sets which are found to have considerable accuracy and low computation complexity (detailed performance in Sect. 5.6).

(1) **STAT35** (35 dimensions): we equally divide one window into five segments, and compute a seven-dimensional feature [19] from each segment, including the mean, maximum, second maximum, minimum, and second minimum absolute values, the standard deviation and the root mean square.

(2) **DSTAT35** (70 dimensions): in addition to STAT35, we also generate a "differential signal" (i.e., the difference between two consecutive readings) from the raw signal and extract a similar seven-dimensional feature from each of its five segments.

(3) **FFT5** (5 dimensions): we do FFT on the raw signal in the whole window and use the coefficients of the first five harmonics as a five-dimensional feature.

(4) **S7FFT5** (35 dimensions): in addition to FFT5, we also extract the same five coefficients from each of two half-size windows and four quarter-size windows. Thus, we obtain 35 dimensions from 7 windows.

(5) **DFFT5** (10 dimensions): the first five FFT coefficients of both raw and differential signals.

We explore a few most common machine learning algorithms, logistic regression (LR) [20] and support vector machine (SVM) [20]. After feature extraction, we manually label the data for training. We find that SVM has higher accuracy with slight more complexity than LR, while both can run fast enough on the phone. So we finally decide to use SVM in experiments. We find it has bump and turn detection accuracies (percentage of correctly labeled samples) around 93%.

We have also tried some threshold-based methods on temporal [21] and frequency-domain [22] features, but find it is impossible to set universally effective thresholds, and the frequency power densities by hand movements can be very similar to those of landmarks. Thus, they are not sufficiently robust.

5.5.3 Prediction and Rollback

The reliability of landmark detection depends on the "completeness" of the signal. If the window covers the full duration of passing a landmark, more numbers of distinctive features can be extracted, and the detection would be more reliable. In reality, this may not always be possible. The landmark detection is repeated at certain intervals, but many intervals may not be precisely aligned with complete landmark-passing durations. One naive solution is to wait until the passing has completed. Thus, more features can be extracted for reliable detection. However, this inevitably increases tracking latency and causes jitters in location estimation and display, adversely impacting user experience.

We use a simple prediction technique to make decisions based on data from such partial durations. To identify whether a car is passing a landmark at time t, assume that the signal spanning from $t - \tau$ to $t + \tau$ covering the full 2τ landmark-passing duration is needed for best results. At any time t, we use data in window $[t - 2\tau, t]$ to do the detection. The results are used by the real-time tracking component to estimate the vehicle location. At time $t + \tau$, the data of full landmark-passing duration become available. We classify data in $[t - \tau, t + \tau]$ and verify if the prediction made at t is correct. Nothing needs to be done if it is. If it was wrong, we rollback all the states in the tracking component to t and repeat the computation with the correct detection to re-estimate the location.

This simple technique is based on the observation that most of the time the vehicle is driving straight and landmarks are rare events. Thus, the prediction remains correct most of the time (i.e., during straight driving), and mistakes/rollbacks happen only occasionally (i.e., when a landmark is encountered). From our experiments, rollbacks happen in a small fraction ($\sim$10%) of the time. Thus, we ensure low latency most of the time because there is no waiting, while preserving detection accuracy through occasional rollback, which incurs more computation but is found to have acceptable latency ($0.05 \sim 0.2$ s) (Sect. 5.6).

5.6 Performance

We implement VeTrack on iOS 6/7/8, so it can run on iPhone 4/4s/5/5s/6. Our code contains a combination of C, C++ for algorithms and Objective C for sensor and GUI operations. A sensor data collector sends continuous data to landmark detectors to produce detection results. Then, the real-time tracking component uses such output to estimate the vehicle's location, which is displayed on the screen. The initialization (e.g., loading map data) takes less than 0.5 s. Sensors are sampled at 50 Hz and the particle states are evolved at the same intervals (20 ms). Since each landmark lasts for many 20 ms intervals, the detectors classify the landmark state once every 10 samples (i.e., every 0.2 s), which reduces computing burden.

We conduct experiments in three underground parking lots: a 250 m × 90 m one in an office building, a 180 m × 50 m one in a university campus, and a 3-level 120 m × 80 m one in a shopping mall. Before the experiments, we have measured and drawn their floor plans (shown in Fig. 5.10). There are 298, 79, 423 parking spots, 19, 12, 10 bumps, 10, 11, 27 turns and 4, 2, 6 slopes, respectively.

For each parking lot, we collect 20 separate trajectories each starting from the entrance to one of the parking spots (shown in Fig. 5.10) for inertial sensor data at different poses. The average driving time for trajectories is 2 ∼ 3 min, and the longest one 4.5 min. Exemplar trajectories to five test spots are illustrated in Fig. 5.11.

For all three lots, we use a mould to hold 4 iPhones with four different poses: horizontal, lean, vertical, and box (Fig. 5.12a). To further test the performance and robustness of our system, we use four more iPhones for the challenging 3-level parking lot with one in driver's right pants' pocket, one in a bag on a seat and two held in hand. The one in pocket is subject to continuous gas/brake pedal actions by the driver, while the one in bag to vehicle movements. Once in a while, one handheld phone is picked up and put down on the user's thigh, causing Z-axis accelerations similar to those by bumps; the other is picked up from and laid down to adjacent seat, causing Z-axis angular changes similar as those by turns. These eight poses hopefully cover all common driving scenarios. The UI of VeTrack is shown in Fig. 5.12b.

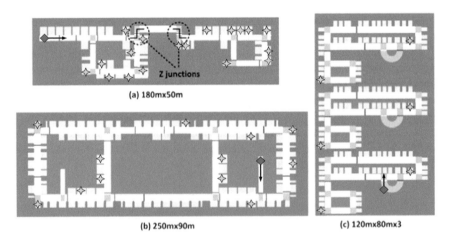

(a) 180mx50m

(b) 250mx90m

(c) 120mx80mx3

Fig. 5.10 Floor maps of three underground parking lots: **a** university campus: 180 m × 50 m with 79 parking spots, 12 bumps and 11 turns. **b** office building: 250 m × 90 m with 298 parking spots, 19 bumps and 10 turns. **c** shopping mall: 3-level 120 m × 80 m with 423 parking spots, 10 bumps and 27 turns. The chosen parking spots and entrance are marked for each lot

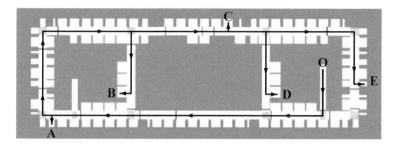

Fig. 5.11 Driving trajectories and test spots. Each trajectory begins at the entrance O and ends at one of the test spots (A to E)

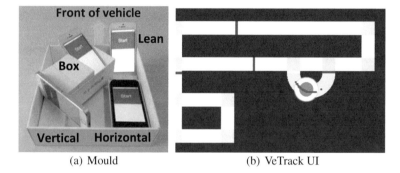

(a) Mould   (b) VeTrack UI

Fig. 5.12 Mould and VeTrack UI

We use video to obtain the ground truth of vehicle location over time. During the course of driving, one person holds an iPad parallel to the vehicle's heading direction to record videos from the passenger window. After driving, we manually examine the video frame by frame to find when the vehicle passed distinctive objects (e.g., pillars) with known locations on the map. Such frames have those objects in the middle of the image, and thus the error is bounded by 0.5 vehicle length and usually much better.

To align inertial data and video collected from different devices temporally, we first synchronize the time on all the iPhones and iPad. Then, different people holding different devices will start the data collecting/recording applications at the same time. These operations establish the correspondence of data in the time series of different devices.

The spatial distribution of real-time tracking errors on a garage map with three bumps and eight turns is shown in Fig. 5.13. Each circle has a number, the error averaged over different traces and poses for that location. We observe that in general the error grows on straight paths and is reduced after encountering landmarks (e.g., from 4.9 m after a corner A, growing to 7.9 m then reduced to 4.6 m after a bump B; 9.7 m at C before a corner to 3.9 m at D).

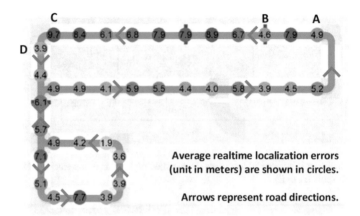

Fig. 5.13 Average real-time tracking errors on different garage locations

5.7 Discussion

Generalization of techniques. The real-time tracking problem itself is quite specific. However, the shadow trajectory tracing and 2D phone pose estimation techniques are essential to model and infer vehicle dynamics where arbitrary phone pose or special driving conditions (e.g., slopes or even slanted driving on slopes) exist. Thus, the benefits are general to phone-vehicular applications, not just underground navigation.

Landmark detection. Although existing work [21, 23] detects landmarks for drivers (e.g., bumps and potholes on road), they largely rely on training thresholds of accelerations at vertical axis, and thus they cannot handle phones with hand movements in car. In comparison, we design certain features manually for machine learning techniques, which is more robust to different road conditions and hand movements. However, those features might not be the optimal under all circumstances; more efficient features specific to different environments may exist. We plan to investigate unsupervised feature learning [24] to automatically devise features for better performance and generality.

Gravity API. In our shadow tracing algorithm, we use the gravity API to obtain the horizontal acceleration from phone's acceleration vector. However, we observe that acute accelerations can pollute gravity estimation, i.e., it remains stable with fixed phone pose during driving, but suffers large disturbances with bumps and hand movements. Thus, we propose landmark detection techniques to identify hand movements and calibrate vehicle's position. We will work on accurate and real-time estimation of phone's attitude in future work.

Stationary or reverse conditions. There are certain movement patterns not yet considered in this work: when the parking lot is congested, the vehicle may exhibit stop-and-go movements with long stationary periods; drivers may back up the vehicle into parking spaces. We plan to add stationary and reverse detection algorithms so that these conditions can be properly recognized and handled within the real-time tracking component.

Mapping the parking structures. Many indoor localization applications, including VeTrack, rely on the availability of floor maps. One can conduct business negotiations with the garage operators for the map, or manually measure for the map and landmark locations. We find that we were able to measure such data within $2 \sim 3$ h in different garages. Although it is a one-time effort with long-lasting benefits, such efforts should be minimized ideally. Using smartphone inertial or vehicle OBD sensors, one can obtain the vehicle trajectory. Our recent work [25] can construct complete garage maps given enough numbers of such trajectories, thus eliminating the need for manual survey.

5.8 Related Work

Phone pose estimation. Existing work [10, 11, 26] estimates the 3D pose of the phone. The latest one, A^3 [14], detects high confidence compass and accelerometer measurements to calibrate accumulative gyroscope errors. The typical approach [10] in vehicular applications is to use the gravity direction as the Z-axis of the vehicle, assuming it is on level ground; gyroscope is used to determine whether the vehicle is driving straight; and the direction of maximum acceleration is assumed to be the Y-axis of the vehicle. As explained in Sect. 5.3, it cannot handle vehicles on a slope, and the direction of maximum acceleration may not be vehicle forwarding direction. The estimation also requires long time of unchanged pose, unsuitable under frequent disturbances.

Landmark detection. Distinctive data patterns in different sensing modalities of smartphones have been exploited for purposes including indoor localization [9, 27]. Similarly, VeTrack detects distinctive inertial sensor patterns by road conditions (e.g., bumps and turns) to calibrate the location estimation. Its algorithms are designed specifically for robustness against noises and disturbances on inertial data from indoor driving.

Robotic localization. SLAM is a popular technique for a robot to acquire a map of its environment while simultaneously localizing itself in this map [28]. It has been adapted for indoor localization leveraging WiFi signals [29]. Unlike SLAM, VeTrack assumes the map is available and determines the vehicle location. This is equivalent to robot localization which finds the pose of a robot relative to a given map.

VeTrack uses the sequential Monte Carlo (SMC) approach on robot localization [15]. But SMC is only a framework: what states are needed to model the dynamics of the physical system, what algorithms are needed to update such states, are all problem dependent. Also, smartphone inertial data have significant noises and disturbances; they do not have high-precision sensors such as laser rangers, high-definition cameras, wheels that can provide accurate measurements for robots. Thus, the state/weight initialization and update have to be carefully designed to produce reasonable results despite low-quality data.

Dead reckoning. Dead reckoning is a well-explored approach that estimates the future location of a moving object (e.g., ground vehicle [30]) based on its past position and speed. Compared with them, VeTrack does not have special, high-precision sensors (e.g., odometer in robotics or radar [30] for ground vehicles), while the required accuracy is much higher than that of aviation.

Dead reckoning has been used for indoor localization using smartphones equipped with multiple inertial sensors [31, 32]. Its main problem is fast error accumulation due to inertial data noises and a lot of work has attempted to mitigate the accumulation. Foot-mounted sensors have been shown effective in reducing the error [33]. Smartphones are more difficult because their poses are unknown and can change. UnLoc [9] replaces GPS with virtual indoor landmarks with unique sensor data patterns for calibration.

To prevent the error accumulation, VeTrack simultaneously harnesses constraints imposed by the map and environment landmarks. Landmark locations most likely remain unchanged for months or even years. The 2D pose estimation handles unknown and possibly changing phone poses. Their output provides calibration opportunities in the SMC framework to minimize error accumulation.

Skeletonization. The process of skeletonization is to peel off a pattern as many pixels as possible without affecting the general shape of the object in a digital binary picture, so as to provide region-based shape features. It is a common preprocessing operation in raster-to-vector conversion or in pattern recognition. There are three major skeletonization techniques: detecting ridges in distance map of the boundary points [34]; calculating the Voronoi diagram generated by the boundary points [16]; and the layer-by-layer erosion called thinning method [17]. We observe that there are always superfluous "branches" for skeletons via distance map or Voronoi diagram, and those mistakes are difficult to remove. Thus, we finally choose a robust thinning method to extract road skeletons.

Estimation of vehicle states. There have been many research efforts using smartphones' embedded sensors to monitor the states of vehicles (e.g., dangerous driving alert [7] and CarSafe [35]); sense driver phone use (e.g., car speaker [23]); inspect the road anomaly or conditions (e.g., Pothole Patrol [21]); and detect traffic accidents (Nericell [26] and WreckWatch [36]). The vehicle speed is a critical input in many such applications. While it is easy to calculate the speed using GPS outdoors [37], the signal can be weak or even unavailable for indoor parking lots. Some alternative solutions leverage the phone's signal strength to estimate the vehicle speed [38]. VeTrack [39] uses inertial data only, and thus it works without any RF signal or extra sensor instrumentation.

5.9 Conclusions

In this chapter, we describe VeTrack which tracks a vehicle's location in real time and records its final parking location. It does not depend on GPS or WiFi signals which may be unavailable, or additional sensors to instrument the indoor environment. VeTrack uses only inertial data, and all sensing/computing happen locally on the phone. It uses a novel shadow trajectory tracing method to convert smartphone movements to vehicle ones. It also detects landmarks such as speed bumps and turns robustly. A probabilistic framework estimates its location under constraints from detected landmarks and garage maps. It also utilizes a 1D skeleton road model to greatly reduce the computing complexity.

Prototype experiments in three parking structures and with several drivers, vehicle make/models have shown that VeTrack can track the vehicle location around a few parking spaces, with negligible latency most of the time. Thus, it provides critical indoor location for universal location awareness of drivers. Currently, VeTrack still has quite some limitations, such as manual feature design, simultaneous disturbances as discussed previously. We plan to further investigate along these directions to make it mature and practical in the real world.

References

1. P. Bahl, V.N. Padmanabhan, RADAR: an in-building RF-based user location and tracking system, in *IEEE INFOCOM* (2000)
2. M. Youssef, A. Agrawala, The horus wlan location determination system, in *ACM MobiSys* (2005)
3. V. Otsason, A. Varshavsky, A. LaMarca, E. De Lara, Accurate gsm indoor localization, in *International Conference on UbiComp, Ubiquitous Computing*, vol. 2005 (Springer, 2005), pp. 141–158
4. SFpark, http://sfpark.org/how-it-works/the-sensors/
5. Parking sensors mesh network, http://www.streetline.com/parking-analytics/parking-sensors-mesh-network/
6. S. Nawaz, C. Efstratiou, C. Mascolo, Parksense: a smartphone based sensing system for on-street parking, in *Proceedings of the 19th Annual International Conference on Mobile Computing & Networking*. ser. MobiCom '13 (ACM, New York, USA, 2013), pp. 75–86. https://doi.org/10.1145/2500423.2500438
7. J. Lindqvist, J. Hong, Undistracted driving: a mobile phone that doesn't distract, in *Proceedings of the 12th Workshop on Mobile Computing Systems and Applications*, ser. HotMobile '11 (ACM, New York, USA, 2011), pp. 70–75. https://doi.org/10.1145/2184489.2184504
8. A. Thiagarajan, J. Biagioni, T. Gerlich, J. Eriksson, Cooperative transit tracking using smartphones, in *Proceedings of the 8th ACM Conference on Embedded Networked Sensor Systems*. ser. SenSys '10 (ACM, New York, USA, 2010), pp. 85–98. https://doi.org/10.1145/1869983.1869993
9. H. Wang, S. Sen, A. Elgohary, M. Farid, M. Youssef, R.R. Choudhury, No need to war-drive: unsupervised indoor localization, in *ACM MobiSys* (2012), pp. 197–210

10. Y. Wang, J. Yang, H. Liu, Y. Chen, M. Gruteser, R.P. Martin, Sensing vehicle dynamics for determining driver phone use, in *Proceeding of the 11th Annual International Conference on Mobile Systems, Applications, and Services.* ser. MobiSys '13 (ACM, New York, USA, 2013), pp. 41–54. https://doi.org/10.1145/2462456.2464447
11. H. Han, J. Yu, H. Zhu, Y. Chen, J. Yang, Y. Zhu, G. Xue, M. Li, Senspeed: sensing driving conditions to estimate vehicle speed in urban environments, in *IEEE INFOCOM* (2014)
12. M. Zhao, R. Gao, J. Zhu, T. Ye, F. Ye, Y. Wang, K. Bian, G. Luo, M. Zhang, Veloc: finding your car in the parking lot, in *Proceedings of the 12th ACM Conference on Embedded Network Sensor Systems* (ACM, 2014), pp. 346–347
13. Apple Developer Center, https://developer.apple.com/
14. P. Zhou, M. Li, G. Shen, Use it free: instantly knowing your phone attitude, in *ACM MobiCom* (2014), pp. 605–616
15. S. Thrun, W. Burgard, D. Fox et al., *Probabilistic Robotics*, vol. 1. (MIT press Cambridge, 2005)
16. M. de Berg et al., *Computational Geometry*, vol. 2. (Springer, 2000)
17. Zhang-suen thinning algorithm, http://rosettacode.org/wiki/Zhang-Suen_thinning_algorithm/
18. Y. Tian, R. Gao, K. Bian, F. Ye, T. Wang, Y. Wang, X. Li, Towards ubiquitous indoor localization service leveraging environmental physical features, in *IEEE INFOCOM* (2014), pp. 55–63
19. S. Preece, J. Goulermas, L. Kenney, D. Howard, A comparison of feature extraction methods for the classification of dynamic activities from accelerometer data. IEEE Trans. Biomed. Eng. (2009)
20. C.M. Bishop et al., *Pattern Recognition and Machine Learning*, vol. 1. (Springer, New York, 2006)
21. J. Eriksson, L. Girod, B. Hull, R. Newton, S. Madden, H. Balakrishnan, The pothole patrol: using a mobile sensor network for road surface monitoring, in *Proceedings of the 6th International Conference on Mobile Systems, Applications, and Services.* ser. MobiSys '08 (ACM, New York, USA, 2008), pp. 29–39. https://doi.org/10.1145/1378600.1378605
22. K. Li, M. Lu, F. Lu, Q. Lv, L. Shang, D. Maksimovic, Personalized driving behavior monitoring and analysis for emerging hybrid vehicles. Pervasive Comput (2012)
23. J. Yang, S. Sidhom, G. Chandrasekaran, T. Vu, H. Liu, N. Cecan, Y. Chen, M. Gruteser, R.P. Martin, Sensing driver phone use with acoustic ranging through car speakers. IEEE Trans Mobile Comput **11**(9), 1426–1440 (2012)
24. G. Hinton, S. Osindero, Y.-W. Teh, A fast learning algorithm for deep belief nets. Neural Comput. **18**(7), 1527–1554 (2006)
25. Q. Zhou, F. Ye, X. Wang, Y. Yang, Automatic construction of garage maps for future vehicle navigation service, in *IEEE ICC* (2016)
26. P. Mohan, V.N. Padmanabhan, R. Ramjee, Nericell: using mobile smartphones for rich monitoring of road and traffic conditions, in *Proceedings of the 6th ACM Conference on Embedded Network Sensor Systems.* ser. SenSys '08 (ACM, New York, USA, 2008), pp. 357–358. https://doi.org/10.1145/1460412.1460450
27. M. Azizyan, I. Constandache, R. Roy Choudhury, Surroundsense: Mobile phone localization via ambience fingerprinting, in *ACM MobiCom* (2009), pp. 261–272
28. M. Montemerlo, S. Thrun, D. Koller, B. Wegbreit, Fastslam: a factored solution to the simultaneous localization and mapping problem, in *AAAI* (2002), pp. 593–598
29. B. Ferris, D. Fox, N.D. Lawrence, Wifi-slam using gaussian process latent variable models, in *IJCAI*, vol. 7 (2007), pp. 2480–2485
30. D.H. Nguyen, J.H. Kay, B.J. Orchard, R.H. Whiting, Classification and tracking of moving ground vehicles. Lincoln Lab. J. **13**(2), 275–308 (2002)
31. A. Rai, K.K. Chintalapudi, V.N. Padmanabhan, R. Sen, Zee: zero-effort crowdsourcing for indoor localization, in *ACM MobiCom* (2012), pp. 293–304
32. I. Constandache, X. Bao, M. Azizyan, R.R. Choudhury, Did you see bob?: human localization using mobile phones, in *ACM MobiCom* (2010), pp. 149–160
33. P. Robertson, M. Angermann, B. Krach, Simultaneous localization and mapping for pedestrians using only foot-mounted inertial sensors, in *ACM UbiComp* (2009), pp. 93–96

34. W. Liu, H. Jiang, X. Bai, G. Tan, C. Wang, W. Liu, K. Cai, Distance transform-based skeleton extraction and its applications in sensor networks. IEEE Trans. Parallel Distrib. Syst. **24**(9), 1763–1772 (2013)
35. C.-W. You, N.D. Lane, F. Chen, R. Wang, Z. Chen, T.J. Bao, M. Montes-de Oca, Y. Cheng, M. Lin, L. Torresani, A.T. Campbell, Carsafe app: alerting drowsy and distracted drivers using dual cameras on smartphones, in *Proceeding of the 11th Annual International Conference on Mobile Systems, Applications, and Services*. ser. MobiSys '13 (ACM, New York, USA, 2013), pp. 461–462. https://doi.org/10.1145/2462456.2466711
36. J. White, C. Thompson, H. Turner, B. Dougherty, D.C. Schmidt, Wreckwatch: automatic traffic accident detection and notification with smartphones. Mob. Netw. Appl. **16**(3), 285–303 (2011). https://doi.org/10.1007/s11036-011-0304-8
37. B. Hoh, M. Gruteser, R. Herring, J. Ban, D. Work, J.-C. Herrera, A.M. Bayen, M. Annavaram, Q. Jacobson, Virtual trip lines for distributed privacy-preserving traffic monitoring, in *Proceedings of the 6th International Conference on Mobile Systems, Applications, and Services*. ser. MobiSys '08 (ACM, New York, USA, 2008), pp. 15–28. https://doi.org/10.1145/1378600.1378604
38. G. Chandrasekaran, T. Vu, A. Varshavsky, M. Gruteser, R.P. Martin, J. Yang, Y. Chen, Vehicular speed estimation using received signal strength from mobile phones, in *Proceedings of the 12th ACM International Conference on Ubiquitous Computing*. ser. Ubicomp '10 (ACM, New York, USA, 2010), pp. 237–240. https://doi.org/10.1145/1864349.1864386
39. M. Zhao, T. Ye, R. Gao, F. Ye, Y. Wang, G. Luo, Vetrack: real time vehicle tracking in uninstrumented indoor environments, in *ACM SenSys* (2015), pp. 99–112

Printed in the United States
By Bookmasters